S0-AZT-031

WRITING FOR LITIGATION

EDITORIAL ADVISORS

Vicki Been
Elihu Root Professor of Law
New York University School of Law

Erwin Chemerinsky
Dean and Distinguished Professor of Law
University of California, Irvine, School of Law

Richard A. Epstein
Laurence A. Tisch Professor of Law
New York University School of Law
Peter and Kirsten Bedford Senior Fellow
The Hoover Institution
Senior Lecturer in Law
The University of Chicago

Ronald J. Gilson
Charles J. Meyers Professor of Law and Business
Stanford University
Marc and Eva Stern Professor of Law and Business
Columbia Law School

James E. Krier
Earl Warren DeLano Professor of Law
The University of Michigan Law School

Richard K. Neumann, Jr.
Professor of Law
Hofstra University School of Law

Robert H. Sitkoff
John L. Gray Professor of Law
Harvard Law School

David Alan Sklansky
Professor of Law
University of California at Berkeley School of Law

Kent D. Syverud
Dean and Ethan A. H. Shepley University Professor
Washington University School of Law

Elizabeth Warren
Leo Gottlieb Professor of Law
Harvard Law School

ASPEN COURSEBOOK SERIES

WRITING FOR LITIGATION

Kamela Bridges
The University of Texas School of Law

Wayne Schiess
The University of Texas School of Law

Wolters Kluwer
Law & Business

Copyright © 2011 CCH Incorporated.

Published by Wolters Kluwer Law & Business in New York.

Wolters Kluwer Law & Business serves customers worldwide with CCH, Aspen Publishers, and Kluwer Law International products. (www.wolterskluwerlb.com)

No part of this publication may be reproduced or transmitted in any form or by any means, electronic or mechanical, including photocopy, recording, or utilized by any information storage or retrieval system, without written permission from the publisher. For information about permissions or to request permissions online, visit us at www.wolterskluwerlb.com, or a written request may be faxed to our permissions department at 212-771-0803.

To contact Customer Care, e-mail customer.service@wolterskluwer.com, call 1-800-234-1660, fax 1-800-901-9075, or mail correspondence to:

Wolters Kluwer Law & Business
Attn: Order Department
PO Box 990
Frederick, MD 21705

Printed in the United States of America.

1 2 3 4 5 6 7 8 9 0

ISBN 978-1-4548-0273-0

Library of Congress Cataloging-in-Publication Data

Bridges, Kamela, 1966-
    Writing for litigation / Kamela Bridges, Wayne Schiess.
        p. cm. — (Aspen coursebook series)
    ISBN 978-1-4548-0273-0
1. Legal composition. 2. Pre-trial procedure — United States. 3. Trial practice — United States.
I. Schiess, Wayne, 1963- II. Title.

KF250.B75 2011
808'.06634 — dc22

                                                    2011005938

About Wolters Kluwer Law & Business

Wolters Kluwer Law & Business is a leading global provider of intelligent information and digital solutions for legal and business professionals in key specialty areas, and respected educational resources for professors and law students. Wolters Kluwer Law & Business connects legal and business professionals as well as those in the education market with timely, specialized authoritative content and information-enabled solutions to support success through productivity, accuracy and mobility.

Serving customers worldwide, Wolters Kluwer Law & Business products include those under the Aspen Publishers, CCH, Kluwer Law International, Loislaw, Best Case, ftwilliam.com and MediRegs family of products.

CCH products have been a trusted resource since 1913, and are highly regarded resources for legal, securities, antitrust and trade regulation, government contracting, banking, pension, payroll, employment and labor, and healthcare reimbursement and compliance professionals.

Aspen Publishers products provide essential information to attorneys, business professionals and law students. Written by preeminent authorities, the product line offers analytical and practical information in a range of specialty practice areas from securities law and intellectual property to mergers and acquisitions and pension/benefits. Aspen's trusted legal education resources provide professors and students with high-quality, up-to-date and effective resources for successful instruction and study in all areas of the law.

Kluwer Law International products provide the global business community with reliable international legal information in English. Legal practitioners, corporate counsel and business executives around the world rely on Kluwer Law journals, looseleafs, books, and electronic products for comprehensive information in many areas of international legal practice.

Loislaw is a comprehensive online legal research product providing legal content to law firm practitioners of various specializations. Loislaw provides attorneys with the ability to quickly and efficiently find the necessary legal information they need, when and where they need it, by facilitating access to primary law as well as state-specific law, records, forms and treatises.

Best Case Solutions is the leading bankruptcy software product to the bankruptcy industry. It provides software and workflow tools to flawlessly streamline petition preparation and the electronic filing process, while timely incorporating ever-changing court requirements.

ftwilliam.com offers employee benefits professionals the highest quality plan documents (retirement, welfare and non-qualified) and government forms (5500/PBGC, 1099 and IRS) software at highly competitive prices.

MediRegs products provide integrated health care compliance content and software solutions for professionals in healthcare, higher education and life sciences, including professionals in accounting, law and consulting.

Wolters Kluwer Law & Business, a division of Wolters Kluwer, is headquartered in New York. Wolters Kluwer is a market-leading global information services company focused on professionals.

To John and Joe, who taught me how to practice law;
and to John, Jake, and Joe, who keep trying
to teach me how to live life
— KB

To my friends Mike and Mike
— WS

Summary of Contents

Contents

Contents

Acknowledgements

We are grateful to the people who helped us as this book took shape. We thank colleagues we've had and have at the University of Texas School of Law, who occasionally indulge us in the notion that we might have something to say. We recognize our students, who have shown us what needs to be said. We appreciate those at Aspen, particularly Lynn Churchill and Dana Wilson, for helping us have our say. We value the comments of the anonymous reviewers, who improved what we have to say. Finally, we recognize the generous legal writing community, which is always willing to ponder, debate, and share the best way to say anything remotely related to law.

We also want to acknowledge those who have helped us individually.

From Kamela:

I am grateful to the folks with whom I practiced law, especially Camille Kerr, Joe Latting, John Schwartz, and Alan Waldrop, for teaching me what I know about being a trial lawyer. Any good strategic advice in this book probably originated with them. I appreciate the persistence of Wayne Schiess, who kept after me for years to take on this project. I express my gratitude to Catherine Bridges for the hours of childcare that made working on this book possible. I thank my parents, Pat Bennett and Jack Stroman, for instilling in me the work ethic every good lawyer needs. Finally, my deepest thanks go to my family, John, Jake, and Joe Bridges, for patiently tolerating the grumpiness that envelops a busy mom.

From Wayne:

I am grateful to be named a co-author with Kamela Bridges on this book, and I appreciate her expertise and skill. I am grateful to my friends and family for their encouragement and patience.

WRITING FOR LITIGATION

INTRODUCTION

If variety is the spice of life, then litigation is the international smorgasbord of practicing law. There's endless variety in the types of cases you may handle. One case might involve antitrust claims between corporate giants. Another might involve a collision at an intersection. Yet another might involve a custody dispute. Even if your practice is concentrated in a certain area of law, each case will involve new parties with new stories to tell. For each case, you'll have to learn the facts better than the witnesses and the opinions better than the experts. Litigation is a great field for those who are constantly curious and never want to stop learning.

(If, someday, you are stuck in a ten-hour-long deposition about insurance annuities, you may believe we've misled you. We're sorry. But note we're touting variety over the span of your practice, not on an hour-by-hour basis.)

Once you're working on a particular case, the variety will continue. One day you might be interviewing witnesses. The next day you might be reviewing documents in discovery. (Okay, document review might go on for a few days — quite a few days.) The next day you might be sitting at your computer, composing a document for the case.

"Ahh," you may think, "that's when the monotony will set in." But even when you're sitting at the computer, if you're writing for litigation, the variety will continue. Over the life of a case, you'll write many types of documents. For each document you write, you'll need to understand

- the audience for the document,
- the document's purpose,
- the proper components of the document,
- the strategies that should guide your writing, and
- the general principles of good writing that apply to all litigation documents.

I. AUDIENCE AND PURPOSE

Early in your legal education, you probably studied two types of documents you might write in a litigation practice: legal memoranda and briefs. That study will give you a good foundation for writing in a litigation practice, but it is only a foundation. As the types of documents you write begin to vary, so must your thought processes in preparing the documents.

The audience members for memos and briefs are typically lawyers (some of whom dress in black robes). The audience for your other litigation documents won't be so routine. Sure, sometimes you'll be writing to lawyers. But sometimes you'll be writing to jurors. Sometimes you'll be writing to a client. And what might that client be like? It might be an in-house counsel with a J.D. and an M.B.A., or an immigrant farm worker with an eighth-grade education. You might think you're writing to one lawyer (your opposing counsel) when really you're writing for another lawyer (the judge). Or you might think you're writing to the judge, when your real audience is the media or an insurance company. For each document you write in litigation, you'll need to consider your audience members and how best to communicate with them.

Just as the audience for litigation documents varies, so do the documents' purposes. The purpose behind memos and briefs is to explain the law, either objectively or persuasively. You'll explain the law in some other litigation documents, too, such as motions or client advice letters. But sometimes you'll have an entirely different purpose, such as documenting a deal with your opposing counsel or getting your bills paid. The point is that you shouldn't go on autopilot, writing each document the same way you wrote the last one, without considering the purpose of the document and how best to achieve that purpose.

An author should always consider the audience and purpose for each document. That's true for all types of legal writing, but it's particularly critical when writing litigation documents because your audience and purpose are always changing.

II. COMPONENTS AND STRATEGY

As audiences and purposes vary, so do the components of litigation documents. Often, the components vary by jurisdiction, by substantive legal area, and by local practice. To aid you in drafting the types of documents you'll create in a litigation practice, in this book we've described typical components for many documents. But you'll also see many cautions to check on and adhere to the local rules and practice where your case is pending. We've tried to generalize about litigation practices, but you won't be practicing in a hypothetical jurisdiction. You'll be trying real cases in real courts. Read their rules.

The strategic issues that will confront you in each case will also vary. Sometimes your client's goal will be to settle a case as cheaply as possible. Sometimes your client will be more interested in publicizing an injustice than in obtaining damages. Sometimes your client's concern will not be this particular case, but the effect on the client's business if copycat litigation follows. Thus, we can't tell you the right strategy for every case. But we can — and will — highlight strategic issues you should consider when drafting different documents.

III. Four Writing Principles for All Litigation Documents

Although audiences, purposes, components, and strategies vary, some general principles of effective writing apply no matter the type of litigation document. If you're writing for litigation, you're a professional writer, paid to produce high-level written work. Many lawyers don't realize that. Professional writers take writing seriously, and you should, too. Here are four principles to guide your writing.

A. Make Information Accessible

In any piece of legal writing, you should make the important information as easy to find and understand as possible. This is doubly true in litigation writing, where a client's rights, a client's money, or a client's freedom is on the line. The critical point of a litigation document should be placed so that the reader gets it, and quickly.

Where is that place? Usually, it's up front. This is one of the failings of much litigation writing: the failure to get the important information in front of the reader right away.

It's one of the most common complaints of judges, too. "Get to the point," they say, over and over. Texas Supreme Court Judge Nathan Hecht has pleaded: "Start in the very first sentence with the problem in this case. Put it right up front. Start early. Don't bury it under a lot of verbiage and preliminaries."[1] So we recommend that litigation documents — where appropriate — have a summary up front unless the rules require something else. Perhaps widely accepted tradition dictates something other than a summary at the start of a document. If so, question that tradition and abandon it if it won't break the rules or hurt your case.

---

1. Nathan Hecht, as quoted in Bryan A. Garner, *Judges on Effective Writing: The Importance of Plain Language*, 73 Mich. B.J. 326, 326 (1994).

But making information accessible means more than putting a summary up front. It means organizing the text at the large scale and at the small scale. Whenever possible, apply these general principles:

- Name and format documents in a way that makes their purpose obvious.
- Use headings and subheadings for the parts of documents, so the reader can skim easily and still grasp what's going on in the document.
- Use thesis sentences and transitions to show relationships between paragraphs.
- Connect sentences to each other so that the writing flows smoothly.
- Use lists to show order and to highlight key information.

We have tried to follow these principles in the text of this book.

B. Avoid Hyperformal, Pompous Legalese

What we mean by this is that too much litigation writing is stuffy, overly formal, and downright pompous. Don't follow that example. Wherever you can, cut fluff, cut Latin, cut old-fashioned words, and cut useless jargon. Although you must first master the legal language, we urge you to then use clear, modern English whenever you can.

This text is written in a conversational style that may not be appropriate for every litigation document you write. We've used the plural, first-person pronoun ("we") and contractions, for example. That's because our audience — students and new lawyers — is different from the audience for your litigation documents. Our purpose is different as well; we're here to teach, not to persuade or argue. As we've said in this chapter, good writers always consider audience and purpose. In your litigation writing, strive to find a natural voice that is conversational, comfortable, and suited to your audience and purpose.

Here's some advice for the novice litigation writer: You might be working from a form document that contains archaic legalese, and for various reasons you might decide to leave some legalese unchanged. For example, it might not be cost effective to take the time necessary to change the language, or your supervisor may prefer the traditional legalese. In those cases, you might need to stick with the legalese.[2] Even in those circumstances, you might also take advantage of some recent research showing that a majority of judges prefer a modern, direct writing style without legalese.[3] While you may think that your supervisor wants it the old way, that may be because your supervisor believes that judges want it that way. Confronted with research showing that judges, too,

---

2. *See* Wayne Schiess, *When Your Boss Wants It the Old Way*, 12 Scribes J. Leg. Writing, 163, 165–66 (2008–2009); Wayne Schiess, *What to Do When a Student Says "My Boss Won't Let Me Write Like That,"* 11 Persps.: Teaching Leg. Research & Writing 113, 114 (2003).

3. Sean Flammer, *Persuading Judges: An Empirical Analysis of Writing Style, Persuasion, and the Use of Plain English*, 16 Leg. Writing 183 (2010).

prefer clear, modern English, your supervisor may allow you to revise to satisfy your audience.

C. Consult Writing Sources

Journalists — who know they are professional writers — have style manuals on their desks. Book editors — all of whom are writing professionals — have dictionaries and usage manuals handy. And technical writers of all sorts — from those who write corporate newsletters and informative magazine articles to those who publish instruction manuals — would not presume to work without access to guides, references, and writing sources. But too many lawyers do.

Think of yourself as a professional writer because you are one. Remember that professional writers stay up on their craft. And when professional writers have a question about punctuation or word usage or writing style, they don't guess. They look it up.

Here are some excellent sources for all litigation writing.

Two Good Legal-Writing References. These are books you don't read straight through; they're for looking things up. Keep them near your desk and consult them every time you have a question.

- Bryan A. Garner, *The Redbook: A Manual on Legal Style* (2d ed., Thompson/West 2006).
- Texas Law Review, *Manual on Usage and Style* (11th ed., Tex. L. Rev. Assn. 2008).

Two General Legal-Writing Style Guides. Do read these books straight through; they're excellent guides to contemporary legal-writing style — how to phrase clear sentences, how to eliminate legalistic tone, and how to avoid common grammar and punctuation problems.

- Richard C. Wydick, *Plain English for Lawyers* (5th ed., Carolina Academic Press 2005).
- Tom Goldstein & Jethro K. Lieberman, *The Lawyer's Guide to Writing Well* (2d ed., U. of Cal. Press 2002).

Three Good Litigation-Writing Guides. These books are aimed at litigation practice and are excellent for the beginner and for the experienced lawyer who wants to improve. None takes a document-by-document approach, as we do here, but all three are good.

- Steven D. Stark, *Writing to Win: The Legal Writer* (Doubleday 1999).
- Irwin Alterman, *Plain and Accurate Style in Court Papers* (ALI-ABA 1987).
- Kenneth F. Oettle, *Making Your Point: A Practical Guide to Persuasive Legal Writing* (ALM Publg. 2007).

D. Produce Neat, Attractive Documents

Most lawyers can't afford to have their documents professionally printed, but none of us are using typewriters, either. So take advantage of modern word-processing and desktop-publishing technologies, which allow you to produce neat, clean, and well-designed documents. Entire books could be and have been written on document design, and though much of that advice has limited application to litigation documents, there is still much a lawyer can learn. Here are two pieces of general advice, followed by some broad generalizations about litigation-document design.

First, read up on document design. Here are three sources we recommend.

Ruth Anne Robbins, *Painting with Print: Incorporating Concepts of Typographical and Layout Design into the Text of Legal Writing Documents*, 2 J. ALWD 108 (2004).

- This article makes the case that textual format and layout can enhance readability and persuasiveness and that lawyers have much to learn in this area.

Matthew Butterick, *Typography for Lawyers: Essential Tools for Polished and Persuasive Documents* (Jones McClure 2010).

- This book presents guidance on document design from a practicing litigator who went to design school.

Robin Williams, *The PC Is Not a Typewriter* (Peachpit Press 1995).

- This simple and entertaining book will help you abandon ineffective layout and typographic habits that are vestiges of the typewriter.

No one expects you to create a motion that looks like an advertising-industry newsletter. But knowing the basics can help you create documents that invite the reader in.

Second, pay attention to what you see. As you read and review litigation documents, or even other written work, take notice of designs, layouts, and formats that work well. Then experiment with them. Master your word processor and learn to create documents that look professionally designed.

Now, some general advice.

Text Justification. Most professionally printed text, as in books, magazines, and brochures, is fully justified—it has neat, vertical margins on the left and right. The text in this book, for example, is fully justified, as is the text in most books. When the full justification is done well, the text looks professional.

The problem for lawyers preparing litigation documents is that we are using word-processing software that is not nearly as sophisticated as the software used for professionally printed documents. Typical word processors aren't as adept at handling the word spacing necessary to produce good-looking, justified text. So when lawyers use full justification, the text often has odd gaps and spaces. You're probably familiar with the result:

The fully justified text tends to look like this, with
some larger spaces and some smaller spaces.
It   looks   odd   and   unprofessional.

Besides the odd look, fully justified text in a word-processed document tends to be harder to read — the odd gaps and spaces slow the reader down.[4] That's why, in documents created with basic word-processing software, left-aligned text, with a ragged right margin, is more readable. We therefore generally recommend left-aligned text for litigation documents.[5]

If you really like the look of fully justified text, you'll need to take extra time and effort in preparing your document:

- Turn on the function to hyphenate words on the right margin, but beware, the software doesn't always know what it's doing. It may want to break the word "newsletter" into "new" and "sletter," for example.
- Hyphenate words on the right margin manually. It can be tedious, though.
- Adjust your line length (margins) and font size.[6] Common sense should tell you that a long line with a small font will be easier to fully justify. But small fonts and long lines aren't usually desirable in litigation documents.

The hassles and headaches of these additional tasks are the main reason we, and the experts, recommend leaving your document left-aligned.[7]

Centered text, even for headings and subheadings, is also falling out of favor. It's still fine to center the title of a document, but for headings, the left margin is preferable.

Fonts. You should know the difference between a serif font and a sans-serif font. Times New Roman and Century Schoolbook are serif fonts because the letters have small extensions, or serifs, at the ends of the strokes. Arial and Verdana are sans-serif fonts because they have no serifs.

Using two fonts in one document is acceptable, although the advice is to combine fonts that are traditional yet distinct, specifically a serif font for topic headings and a sans-serif font for explanatory headings and body text.

And you should know that if you create an entire document — especially a long one — with a sans-serif type for the body text, you will give it an informal or "light" feel. For litigation documents, a serif font is usually best for the body text.

No Courier.

---

4. Robin Williams, *The PC Is Not a Typewriter* 46 (Peachpit Press 1995).
5. *See* Matthew Butterick, www.TypographyForLawyers.com, under "Justified text."
6. Williams, *supra* note 4, at 46.
7. *Id.* at 45; Matthew Butterick, www.TypographyForLawyers.com, under "Justified text."

White Space. Top and bottom margins for litigation documents should be 1 inch. Left and right margins should be at least 1 inch, and some recommend 1.25 inches to give documents a less crowded look. In fact, some courts are now requiring lawyers to use 1.25-inch left and right margins.

Reader Aids. Contemporary litigation documents should use:

Headings, as in this text, both standard headings above the text and in-line headings.

Enumeration, like this:

> The important factors are (1) the audience, (2) the document's purpose, and (3) the strategic considerations for the document.

Tabulation, like this:

> The important factors are
>
> - the audience
> - the document's purpose
> - the strategic considerations for the document

Enumeration with tabulation, like this:

> The important factors are
>
> (1) the audience,
> (2) the document's purpose, and
> (3) the strategic considerations for the document.

Modern litigation documents should also use images, graphics, text boxes, and tables when appropriate.

These design principles are fairly rough, and we've been presented them quickly. They may not make or break your case, but they will make your documents easier to read and pleasant to look at. Those are worth something when the reader is a busy judge or a hostile opposing counsel.

IV. WRITING LIKE A LAWYER

One final and key aspect of taking your writing seriously is using your skills as a lawyer for every document you write. Sure, you could find forms for many of the types of documents you'll write in litigation. And you could mindlessly fill in those forms. But the forms will never be tailored to your case. The forms won't know who you are writing to or why you are writing. The forms will leave gaping holes for the key parts of the documents, with generic directions like, "describe facts leading to cause of action for negligence." And the forms will have no idea whether, given your particular case, the best strategy is to make that description as detailed or as bare bones as possible. You, the lawyer, must determine how best to accomplish your client's goals with every document you write.

Because litigation writing can't be boiled down to a few forms, we will provide guidance for drafting the variety of documents you'll create in a litigation practice. This text will walk you through many of the documents you are likely to write during the life of a case, from the engagement letter with your client at the beginning to the jury instructions at the end. For each type of document, we'll discuss who your likely audience members will be. We'll talk about the possible purposes of the document, which may not always be the purposes you would initially assume. We'll walk through the components of the document to give you some idea of what your document should contain. And we'll suggest some strategic issues you should consider as you write.

Onward, then, to the variety that awaits you — the professional writer.

1

ENGAGEMENT LETTERS

Before you write anything for a case, you'll need a client, and your agreement to represent that client ought to be in writing. That writing may take the form of a traditional contract, but lawyers often use engagement letters to document the terms of their agreements with their clients.

I. AUDIENCE

The obvious audience member for your engagement letter is your client. Remember that while you may sign countless engagement letters over the life of your career, signing an engagement letter — in other words, hiring a lawyer — may be a momentous (and likely unwelcome) occasion for your client. To make the occasion as pain free as possible, write a letter that's easily understood.

Unfortunately, your client won't always be the sole audience member for your engagement letter. If the attorney and the client disagree about what representation was undertaken — what expenses the client was to pay, or other details of the engagement — new audience members will be inspecting the engagement letter. A judge, jurors, or a mediator or arbitrator may use the letter to determine the lawyer's and client's rights and responsibilities. However, a well-written engagement letter can keep disagreements from turning into disputes by spelling out the answers.

II. PURPOSE

The purpose of the engagement letter is to document the terms of your relationship with your client — your attorney-client relationship. To create a clear framework for that relationship, the engagement letter should clearly set out your client's responsibilities and your responsibilities.

The client's responsibilities may include cooperation with counsel, prompt responses to requests for information, and timely payment of bills. The attorney's main responsibilities are to handle the client's matter competently and to communicate with the client about the matter. The letter should spell out what you are undertaking to do — and, sometimes, what you are *not* undertaking to do. You must specify the scope of your representation of the client. And since this is litigation, where results are never certain, the letter should not guarantee a successful outcome.

If your jurisdiction requires that a contract between a lawyer and a client be in writing, another purpose of your letter is to satisfy that requirement. Check the professional responsibility rules for your jurisdiction to make sure you are in compliance.

III. COMPONENTS OF AN ENGAGEMENT LETTER

While an engagement letter is called a "letter," it is really a contract between a client and a lawyer. As such, it can take the form of a contract or a letter. If you use a letter format, the law firm will be identified in the stationery letterhead and the client will be identified in the address line. The letter should be dated and contain a reference ("re:") line identifying the subject of the letter. If the engagement letter is written in contract form, the parties to the contract will be identified in its body, and the date will appear with the signature lines at the end. In the body of the letter or contract, consider including the following components, although the order in which they are addressed can vary.

A. Identification of the Client

If you are representing an individual, the client's name in the addressee line of the letter is probably enough. But in other situations you may need to identify the specific client. For example, a letter addressed to a company employee might need to identify the company, not the employee, as the client. If you are undertaking to represent multiple parties, consider and address any potential conflict-of-interest issues according to your professional responsibility rules.

B. Description of the Matter the Lawyer Is Agreeing to Handle

Be as specific as possible here. For example, if you are agreeing to represent a client in a discrimination claim against the client's employer, does that mean you will represent the client during internal grievance proceedings at the company? Will you take the steps necessary to exhaust the client's administrative remedies? Will you help the client obtain unemployment benefits? Spell out what you are and are not undertaking to do.

For example, you might say this:

Martin & Associates P.C. will represent you in your lawsuit against Apple Tree Foods for violation of the Americans with Disabilities Act and in any appeal arising from this suit. This engagement letter covers only the lawsuit filed in court against Apple Tree Foods. It does not include any internal complaint you may make within Apple Tree Foods or claim you may file with any governmental agency complaining about the discrimination or seeking benefits.

C. List of the Client's Responsibilities

Think of what you might need from the client and include it here. For example, you'll need the client to give you complete and accurate information, to notify you if the client moves or changes phone numbers, to respond promptly to requests for information, and to cooperate with you in scheduling matters. Spell out these responsibilities — and maybe even highlight them in some way.

Writing Tip — Emphasizing Text

Highlighting language in an engagement letter or contract means finding ways to emphasize text.

RESIST THE TEMPTATION TO USE ALL CAPITALS FOR EMPHASIS.

Besides being a vestige of the typewriter and being rather hard to read, uppercase text can come across as shouting. You have other options for emphasis:

- Boldface
- Italics
- Contrasting fonts
- Indentation
- Text boxes

Often, to be certain that text is emphasized, you can use several techniques at once. In the following example, key information is presented in boldface, italics, and indentation to create emphasis:

It is important that we be able to reach you to discuss developments in your case. You have provided us with an address, telephone number, and cell phone number at which you can be reached.

If any of your contact information changes, you must provide us with the new information promptly.

D. List of the Lawyer's Responsibilities

You will have a set of responsibilities by virtue of the attorney-client relationship. You will have to keep the client informed. You will have to involve the client in decisions. You will have to decline representation adverse to the client.

You will have to return the client's files upon request. Listing your obligations here demonstrates balance in the agreement.

E. Explanation of How the Lawyer Will Be Compensated

The following are examples of the significant details to address in the section on compensation:

- If compensation is on an hourly basis, what rates will you charge? Give the rates for everyone you plan to have work on the matter, as well as the ranges of rates for others who might become involved.
- In what increments will time be billed?
- How often will the client be billed?
- Are rates raised annually?
- If compensation is on a contingency-fee basis, will your share come from the amount of a judgment or from the amount collected?
- In a contingent-fee case, how will you be compensated if the client agrees to a settlement that involves a payout over time?
- In a contingent-fee case, will the contingency percentage increase if there is an appeal?

Considering all the possibilities and addressing them in advance can prevent future disputes.

F. List of Additional Expenses the Client Will Be Expected to Pay

Rather than just stating that the client will be expected to pay expenses, enumerate them:

- Travel expenses
- Computerized legal research fees
- Expert witness fees
- Filing fees
- Copying charges
- Postage
- Meals

If the case is being handled on a contingency-fee basis, the letter should address whether you expect the client to pay in advance for these expenses or whether you will instead subtract them from any recovery. If the expenses are taken out of the recovery, the letter should also address whether you will subtract them before or after you calculate your contingency fee. If the expense isn't listed, don't expect the client to pay it.

G. Explanation of How a Retainer Fee Will Be Used

Explain whether the retainer fee is a true retainer — paid to the lawyer just for taking the case and the lawyer's to keep even if the case settles the next day — or if it is really an advance payment of fees, so that future bills will be drawn against it until it's depleted. (Note that if it is an advance payment, you may be required to keep the funds in a client trust account until you earn them.)

H. Statement That Either Party Can End the Relationship

You need to be able to end your representation of an uncooperative client, and your client always has the right to fire you.

I. Reminder That You Cannot Guarantee the Outcome in the Case

Sometimes a lawyer's enthusiasm for the client's case can sound like a guaranteed win. Then, when a reasonable settlement offer arrives, the client may balk because settling may not seem like "winning." Or when an excessive verdict is delivered against the client, the client may cry foul. Managing client expectations will be important throughout the case. The engagement letter should contain the first of many warnings that you cannot guarantee a certain outcome.

J. Identification of Whom the Client Can Contact with Complaints

If the client is dissatisfied with your conduct, the client may not know whom to tell. Certainly you would like to hear the complaints directly from the client, but the client might not be comfortable speaking to you about the complaints. Still, it is better to learn of complaints before they turn into grievances or lawsuits. If you work at a law firm, the letter can state the name and contact information for the managing partner. If you work at an agency or other entity, the letter can identify the supervisor in charge. If you work alone, you can list the state bar division that handles complaints about lawyer conduct. You don't want to invite grievances, but providing the contact information demonstrates that you are cooperative and open to feedback. This is certainly preferable to testimony later that the client was dissatisfied for some time but didn't know whom to tell.

K. Explanation of What Is Necessary for Representation to Begin

When will you begin working on the client's matter? When you get the signed engagement letter back? When you receive your retainer fee? When the check clears? Specify at what point you will begin serving as the client's attorney.

L. Explanation of What Is Necessary for You to Represent the Client in Additional Matters

Your client may have multiple matters that could benefit from a lawyer's attention. Without some explanation from you, the client may assume that once the client has hired a lawyer, the lawyer will tend to all such matters.

You don't want your client to assume you are representing that client in every legal matter the client mentions in passing. If you will require a new engagement letter to take on additional matters, say so. Or if you want this engagement letter to cover future matters, specify that you will agree in writing to the scope of any new representation you will undertake for the client.

You can combine your explanation of what is necessary for you to represent the client in additional matters with your statement of the scope of the representation, like this:

Scope of Representation

Bissell & Forrester, LLP will represent Apple Tree Foods in the case styled *Simms v. Apple Tree Foods*; Civil Action No. 11-CV-491; In the United States District Court for the Northern District of Jefferson, and in any appeal arising from this case. This engagement letter covers only the Simms case. If Apple Tree Foods would like Latting & Waldrop to represent it in any other matters, I will be happy to discuss the representation with you. Before we will begin representing you in other matters, Latting & Waldrop and Apple Tree Foods will need to sign a separate engagement letter for each matter.

M. Signatures

If the engagement letter is in letter form, the lawyer's signature will appear in the usual spot. If the engagement letter is in the form of a contract between the client and the law firm (rather than an individual lawyer), put the firm name first, then "By" and the lawyer's name. This will show that the lawyer is signing on behalf of the firm. Below the signature line, create a space for the client to sign, indicating the client's agreement to the letter's terms. Thus, the end of your engagement letter might look like this:

Sincerely,

Eva Richards

Bissell & Forrester, LLP
By: Eva Richards
For the Firm

Agreed:

_____

Carrington Displays, Inc.
By Mike Carrington, President
Date: _____

IV. STRATEGIC CONSIDERATIONS FOR ENGAGEMENT LETTERS

There's a tension present when drafting an engagement letter. You want the client to feel comfortable handing an important matter over to you, and you don't want to scare off the client. But you also want to avoid guaranteeing victory, and you want to protect your own interests in case the attorney-client relationship goes awry. Keep these strategic considerations in mind to navigate that tension.

A. Demonstrate Balance

When drafting an engagement letter, you begin with two strikes against you. Under typical contract-construction law, because you are the person drafting the contract, the contract will be construed against you. (Strike one.) Also, since you are a lawyer, and your client (presumably) is not, the contract will be construed against you. (Strike two.)

A sensible reaction when facing rules of construction that favor the other party might be to take extra care to make sure that every detail to your benefit is spelled out completely: what expenses the client must pay, what day payment is due, what happens if payment is late, and so on. But an onerous-sounding letter that specifies all your client's obligations and guarantees nothing in return may result in strike three: loss of the client.

Hence the tension. You want to spell out the client's obligations while avoiding making guarantees yourself, but you don't want to sound so greedy or disagreeable that you lose the client or make an unfavorable impression on any third party called upon to resolve a dispute between you and the client. A couple of suggestions might help.

First, write the letter in plain English. A simple, understandable letter can help eliminate the need to construe the letter against you because there will be less confusing legalese and fewer ambiguities to resolve. It can also show that you were forthright with the client, which can cut down on the predisposition to favor the nonlawyer.

Writing Tip — Plain English

Writing an engagement letter in plain English can be a challenge. After all, you need certain substantive content to ensure that the client is fully informed and to protect yourself. The substantive content might sometimes require you to convey complex ideas and to use legal terminology. Still, you can often simplify the language of engagement letters by applying these common principles of plain English:

- Keep sentences short — strive for an average sentence length of 20 words or fewer.

- Keep paragraphs short. Long blocks of text are practically asking not to be read.
- If the letter is longer than a page or two, use headings for main sections.
- To highlight key responsibilities, use bulleted lists.
- Minimize insider legal jargon and terms of art — and define and explain the jargon and terms of art you must use.

For further advice on writing legal documents in plain English, see Richard C. Wydick, *Plain English for Lawyers* (5th ed., Carolina Academic Press 2005), and Wayne Schiess, *Preparing Legal Documents Nonlawyers Can Read and Understand* (ABA 2008).

Second, list your obligations to the client. Rather than listing the client's obligations to you and stating only that you will handle the matter but won't guarantee results, spell out what you are promising to do for the client. Don't worry that you will have to take on additional obligations to make the engagement letter seem balanced. Your state's disciplinary rules are going to impose obligations on you whether you state them in the engagement letter or not. For example, the rules may require you to keep the client informed, turn down representation adverse to the client, involve the client in decisions, and return the client's files upon request. Listing these obligations in your engagement letter can demonstrate that your agreement is balanced and reasonable.

B. Talk About the Letter First

A long letter full of abstract language, representations and warranties, and legal terms can be overwhelming to a potential client. When a decision maker evaluates the engagement letter after the fact, a lawyer who insisted that the client sign on the spot can look like a pushy salesperson. So the engagement letter is best preceded by a conversation. You can do this in a couple of ways. You can review the letter in person with the potential client, then ask the potential client to take it and think about it before signing and returning it. Or you can discuss the anticipated contents of the letter with the potential client and then send the letter after the meeting. Consider giving the client a chance to suggest and add terms to the letter; this will increase the likelihood that the arrangement will be perceived as fair. As discussed next, make sure the client understands that the letter must be returned before the engagement begins.

C. Specify When the Engagement Begins

Every lawyer has probably heard the tale. A casual acquaintance or even a stranger strikes up a conversation at a cocktail party. Upon learning that you are a lawyer, the person pours out a tale of woe and asks for your advice. You offer some general suggestions and your business card in case the person wants to hire you. You part ways, wondering if you will ever hear from the potential client again. You do, but it's months later, after the statute of limitations has passed, when the "potential" client asks what you have done in the case.

If your only contact with the potential client is oral, of course, you will have to say in the conversation that you are not undertaking to represent the person yet. If you meet with the client before presenting the engagement letter, tell the client you're not hired until the engagement letter is returned. That means you should not agree to start any action for the client until the letter is returned, or you'll be sending mixed signals about whether you have agreed to represent the client. Then in the engagement letter, specify at what point the client may consider you hired. If you will not begin representing the client until you receive the signed engagement letter, say so. That's the best way to keep yourself from unwittingly gaining a new client.

V. CONCLUSION

A successful engagement letter will satisfy both its audience and its purpose. The client will feel confident handing the legal issue over to you, and the responsibilities will be spelled out so clearly that disputes will be much less likely. For a sample engagement letter, see Appendix A.

2

DEMAND LETTERS

Now that you have a client, your next writing might be to your client's opponent. If you are representing a potential plaintiff, you may need to send a demand letter.

I. AUDIENCE

Your primary audience for a demand letter is, of course, the potential defendant. (If you know the potential defendant is represented by a lawyer for this matter, the letter should instead go to the defendant's lawyer.) That defendant may be an individual or it may be a company or some other entity. The defendant will be the first to read the letter, but don't expect it to be the last. The letter will be passed along to the defendant's lawyer and, in some cases, to its insurance carrier.

You may be passing along the demand letter, too. Since you will frequently send a demand letter as a prerequisite to filing suit, you can expect to attach it as an exhibit to your complaint. There, it may be read by the judge, a law clerk, or potentially even jurors. Your client will read it as well.

II. PURPOSE

Why are you writing the demand letter? The answer is not as easy as it may seem. Your purpose will vary. Sometimes you'll be trying to get the defendant to take some action so a lawsuit won't be necessary. Sometimes you'll hope to get the defendant to settle before you file suit. Sometimes you'll just be giving required notice before initiating a suit. And sometimes you'll be sending a letter to protect your rights, such as in a copyright- or trademark-infringement action.

So there isn't a correct answer to the question of what your purpose is in writing a demand letter. Your purpose may vary from one letter to the next.

For each letter, you'll need to consider what your purpose is with that particular letter and draft your letter accordingly.

III. COMPONENTS OF A DEMAND LETTER

Because your demand is in the form of a letter, it will contain the components of a typical letter: The firm's name and address in the letterhead, the name and address of the person the letter is addressed to, the date, a reference line identifying the subject of the letter, a salutation, and a signature line. The body of the letter should include the following components.

A. Identification of Your Client

The recipient of your letter may not know who you are or why you are writing. Begin with that information. For example, you might say:

> I represent the Estates of Oak Creek. I am writing because the boat sitting on your front lawn violates the Estates of Oak Creek's restrictive covenants.

B. The Demand

While it may seem abrupt to state your demand before providing the background for it, that's the information the reader is most interested in. If your client is asking for a specific dollar amount, go ahead and tell the reader what it is. If your client needs the recipient to take some action, specify what it is. For example,

> Please remove the boat from your property immediately.

Writing Tip — Get to the Point

The idea that you should summarize and put key information up front is one of the most widely recommended practices in legal writing:

> Don't make your reader hang on for the surprise ending. You are not Agatha Christie. Instead, state your conclusion very early in your writing.
>
> — Timothy Perrin, *Better Writing for Lawyers* 98–99 (Law Soc. of Upper Canada 1990).

> State your conclusion on any specific issue at the outset.
>
> — John C. Dernbach, et al., *A Practical Guide to Legal Writing & Legal Method* 153 (2d ed., Fred B. Rothman 1994).

> In each part of your legal analysis, give the bottom line first, plainly and without fanfare.
>
> — Irwin Alterman, *Plain and Accurate Style in Court Papers* 97 (ALI-ABA 1987).

> I have run across [those] who thought this was the way to write reports: Feed out details gradually, "create suspense," save the big news to the last. But this is a poor way to organize a piece of writing . . . .
>
> — Robert Gunning, *The Technique of Clear Writing* 130 (McGraw-Hill 1968).
>
> But it is probably the most often violated principle of legal writing. So if that commentary from the experts doesn't persuade you, consider this comment from a trial lawyer:
>
> When I get a demand letter that starts with background and doesn't give me the dollar amount or the demand up front, I always flip to the end to get that information first. Then I read the letter.

C. Support for the Demand

Next, the letter should explain the support for the demand. If the claim is based on the breach of a contract, identify the contract and the provision violated. If the claim is based on a statute, identify the statute and the facts that show the violation. If the claim is a common law claim, you don't need to cite case law, but you should name the claim and explain the facts supporting it.

Here's how you might explain the support for a demand:

> Your property is located within the Estates of Oak Creek. All property within the Estates of Oak Creek is bound by the Declaration of Restrictive Covenants for the Estates of Oak Creek. Article 5, Paragraph 3 of the Restrictive Covenants states: "No trailers, trailer homes, mobile homes, boats, or non-working vehicles may be parked or stored on the property." The boat sitting on your lawn violates this covenant.

If you are demanding a certain dollar amount, you should demonstrate your client's entitlement to the amount demanded. Explain how you have calculated the amount and what evidence it is based on.

D. Consequences

End your letter by identifying the consequences that will follow if the demand is not met. Be sure to include a deadline so the recipient knows the date by which compliance is required. For example,

> Your boat must be removed from your property by September 9, 2011. If it is not removed by that day, the Estates will file a lawsuit asking the court to order you to remove your boat and to award the Estates its attorneys' fees and costs incurred in filing the suit. We look forward to your prompt compliance.

If your client is demanding a certain dollar amount, explain that the offer to settle for that amount will remain open only until a certain date.

IV. STRATEGIC CONSIDERATIONS FOR DEMAND LETTERS

The various potential audience members and purposes create several strategic considerations when drafting a demand letter.

A. Strategic Considerations Related to Audience

First, if your letter is directed to a nonlawyer, it ought to be intelligible to a nonlawyer. Practice plain English here. Some lawyers try to justify using legalese in a demand letter by saying that sounding like a lawyer will scare the defendant into settling. (It would be an interesting empirical study to find out whether sending a dense, legalese-laden letter scares defendants into settling or sends them running angrily to an attorney.)

But sending a letter full of legalese just isn't necessary. As Steven Stark says, "Anyone who gets a letter with all those names at the top and the fancy printing is going to know it came from a lawyer; you don't need the antiquated language."[1]

Second, if the defendant is represented by a lawyer or is likely to hire one upon receiving your letter, specify your client's legal claim. Although legalese isn't necessary, appropriate legal writing is: A citation to relevant statutes or cases and an explanation of the claim can convince an attorney that your claim is valid. That can go a long way toward convincing the potential defendant to take the claim seriously as well.

Third, because your letter might be sent to the potential defendant's insurer, consider whether you can explain your claim in a way that is likely to invoke insurance coverage. Your client's ultimate interest, after all, is probably in securing a recovery, not just in getting a judgment.

Fourth, because your letter might be seen by a judge, law clerk, or juror, you need to be polite. There's no sense in annoying the decision maker with the first thing you write.

Finally, having your client in the audience may encourage you to write a more aggressive letter than you otherwise would. Your client hired you because you are a bulldog, right? But that aggressive tone might actually be detrimental to your client's interests. Consider explaining to your client why a more measured tone is preferable to ratcheting up the vitriol.

---

1. Steven D. Stark, *Writing to Win: The Legal Writer* 171 (Doubleday 1999).

Writing Tip — Civility

Raise yourself and your client above name calling, sarcasm, and open anger. The American Bar Association Section on Litigation has Guidelines for Conduct that it adopted in 1996, and they contain the following:

> We will practice our profession with a continuing awareness that our role is to zealously advance the legitimate interests of our clients. In our dealings with others we will not reflect the ill feelings of our clients. We will treat all other counsel, parties, and witnesses in a civil and courteous manner, not only in court, but also in all other written and oral communications.

ABA Section of Litigation, *Guidelines for Conduct,* http://www.americanbar.org/ groups/litigation/policy/conduct_guidelines/lawyers_duties.html (accessed Feb. 14, 2011).

Aspire to that.

B. Strategic Considerations Related to Purpose

Because your potential purposes are so varied, you really have to decide what your purpose is to determine the content and tone of your letter. Here are some possibilities.

Prompt the Defendant to Take Action or Settle. You may be writing a demand letter because you really hope you can resolve the matter without litigation. For example, homeowners associations that send out letters about barking dogs or cars on the front lawn *really* don't want to have to sue. If you and your client really don't want to sue, there are a couple of approaches you can take, and they fall on the ends of a spectrum. In *The Redbook*, writing expert Bryan Garner says that typically a demand letter should "goad the adversary to capitulate."[2] That sounds like a fairly aggressive approach, and it may work in some instances.

On the other end of the spectrum, a calm approach may be more likely to bring about a resolution. This approach might be called, "perhaps you didn't realize this was a problem." The calm approach often works because a defendant with its back against the wall may feel it has no choice but to come out swinging, while a defendant approached calmly with potential solutions may at least be willing to talk. As Steven Stark notes in *Writing to Win*, "[I]t is far more difficult to deescalate a fight than it is to escalate one."[3]

You will have to select a tone along this spectrum that is most likely to succeed in your situation. As Garner aptly notes in *The Redbook*, "As a writer, you must get inside the recipient's head to understand what type of approach will

---

2. Bryan A. Garner, *The Redbook: A Manual on Legal Style* 367 (2d ed., Thomson/West 2006).

3. Stark, *supra* note 1, at 239.

succeed."[4] Just keep in mind that a letter calmly laying out the cause of action and the available remedies can be as influential as a letter impugning the defendant or suggesting that the defendant had ill intent.

Document Your Efforts to Resolve the Matter. Here your purpose is similar to prompting the defendant to settle, but not identical. Your goal here is to show that you tried. You may do this to invoke a cost-shifting statute, to set up a claim for attorneys' fees later, or to engender goodwill with the court. If you are making the effort because of a statute that provides an advantage to one who offers to settle before filing suit, be sure you comply with the statute so your client will be able to avail itself of the benefit. If your purpose is only to show that you tried, your tone should be cordial and accommodating. You won't look like you tried to resolve the matter if your letter is threatening or bullying.

Fulfill a Prerequisite to Filing Suit. You may be required to send a demand letter before filing suit. The requirement may be statutory. Consumer protection statutes, for example, frequently require notice before suit is filed. The requirement may be contractual. Loan documents, for example, often require a demand with time to cure the default.

If you are writing a demand letter as a prerequisite to filing suit, be sure to comply strictly with the requirements. If you don't know if a demand is required, research the substantive law. Then follow its requirements.

If your client plans to sue under a contract, read the contract to see if it contains a notice provision. If it does, then follow that provision carefully. It may contain detailed requirements about who must be notified, at what address, and when. It may specify the method of delivery for your notice. Note that a notice provision in a contract may be drafted so that the notice is a prerequisite to suit, but it can also be drafted so that the notice requirement creates a contractual obligation, the breach of which results in a claim for breach of contract.[5] It may be hard to imagine someone filing suit over such a breach, but you do not want to give the defendant a potential counterclaim.

You want your notice to be effective, so comply to the letter with all requirements.

V. OTHER "DOS" AND "DON'TS" FOR DEMAND LETTERS

Your demand letter should do the following:

- Include some detail about what has happened. If you show you've done your homework, you'll have a better chance of being taken seriously. For

---

4. Garner, *supra* note 2, at 367.
5. Tina L. Stark, *Negotiating and Drafting Contract Boilerplate* 470 (ALM Publg. 2003).

example, imagine you are representing a potential plaintiff in an employment discrimination case. If you say only that she was discriminated against, it might not get anyone's attention. But if you can back up your claim with specific examples, the person who gets the letter—who may know nothing about the people involved—will be more likely to take it seriously.

- Make sure any details you include are accurate. If you get any facts wrong, you can be certain they will come back to haunt you later in litigation. Your letter will be good fodder for cross examination of your client. Inconsistencies will hurt your client's credibility.
- Make clear what your client is asking for. Does the client want some action to stop (use of a protected trade secret, for instance)? Does your client want to be reinstated to a position? Does your client want monetary damages? If so, in what amount? Make sure you include your attorneys' fees and other expenses, in case this offer is accepted.
- Provide a deadline. You don't want to sit around wondering if the defendant will meet your demands. Your deadline should give the defendant some time to consider the matter and consult a lawyer but should not leave the time for a response open-ended.
- State what action you will take if the demand is not met by that deadline.
- Send your demand letter by regular mail and by certified mail, return receipt requested (unless, of course, your statute or contract specifies another form of delivery). That way, if the defendant picks up the certified letter, you've got proof of delivery, but if the defendant refuses to pick it up, your regular-mail letter will still reach the defendant.

But don't fall into these traps:

- Don't threaten criminal action to get a settlement. The Model Code of Professional Responsibility prohibits a lawyer from threatening to present criminal charges solely to obtain advantage in a civil matter.[6]
- Don't threaten civil action cavalierly. Although a lawyer's writings in the course of litigation are usually privileged (meaning the lawyer is personally protected from claims such as defamation), the privilege rules are less clear for documents written before a suit is filed. The United States District Court for the District of Massachusetts, for example, denied a motion to dismiss a claim against a law firm based on a demand letter the firm sent.[7] The court said that the firm had not established "that its acts of drafting and sending the letter were privileged because they were taken at a time when litigation was contemplated in good faith and under serious

---

6. ABA Model Code of Professional Responsibility, DR 7-105(A).
7. *Meltzer v. Grant*, 193 F. Supp. 2d 373, 381 (D. Mass. 2002).

consideration."[8] Threatening litigation can also, in limited circumstances, be criminal extortion.[9] So if your client wants you to fire off a letter even though the client is sure it will never actually sue, don't do it.

- Don't send a letter directly to someone you know is represented by counsel. That runs afoul of Model Rule of Professional Conduct 4.2.

VI. CONCLUSION

Because different demand letters can have different purposes, you'll need to carefully consider your client's goal before you begin composing. Then, write a letter that states your client's demands in a civil tone, keeping all the potential audience members for your letter in mind. For a sample demand letter, see Appendix B.

---

8. *Id.*

9. *See, e.g., U.S. v. Sturm*, 870 F.2d 769, 774 (1st Cir. 1989); *State v. Hynes*, 978 A.2d 264, 270 (N.H. 2009).

3

COMPLAINTS

From your client's perspective, the complaint is the chance to tell the world its story. While you are helping your client do that, though, you should also keep in mind certain audience members and more specific purposes.

I. AUDIENCE

The obvious answer to the question "Who is the audience for a complaint?" might not be the correct one. Since you will be filing your complaint at the courthouse, you might assume that a judge will read it. Maybe. Some judges like to read complaints filed in their courts to see what lies ahead. But in other courts, judges don't have the time (or inclination) to look at a case until there's a need to act. Even then, depending on the action requested, the judge might not read the complaint. For example, a judge called upon to decide a motion to dismiss will need to read the complaint. But a judge deciding a summary judgment motion might look at the motion, response, and evidence, and might never look at the complaint. So although the judge might be among your audience members, the complaint may sit in the court's file, unread.

Besides the judge, who else might read your complaint?

- The defendant
- The defendant's attorney
- The judge's law clerk
- Members of the media
- Your client
- The defendant's insurer
- Members of the jury

That's a diverse and potentially large audience, but don't let that distract you from achieving the complaint's primary purpose.

II. PURPOSE

The primary purpose in writing a complaint is to plead a viable claim. You want to file a lawsuit that will survive a motion to dismiss. If that isn't your primary purpose, you may run afoul of Federal Rule of Civil Procedure 11, your state sanctions rule, or ethics rules.

But is pleading a viable claim the only purpose? What else are you trying to accomplish when you write your complaint?

- You might hope to encourage an early settlement offer.
- You might want to persuade the judge that you have a strong case.
- You might seek favorable media attention.
- You might want to satisfy your client's desire to tell its story.
- You might be trying to invoke insurance coverage for your claim.
- You might need to meet a limitations deadline or toll limitations for potential, related claims.

We'll return to these secondary purposes when we address strategic considerations.

III. PRE-SUIT REQUIREMENTS FOR A COMPLAINT

Before considering the pleading requirements for a claim, you should consider whether any pre-suit requirements apply. Pre-suit requirements vary with the jurisdiction, the type of claim, and the particular situation at hand. For example, you need to ask yourself these kinds of questions:

- Is there a statutory requirement that the plaintiff give notice before filing the suit?
- Does a contract require an opportunity to cure any default?
- Does the plaintiff need to exhaust administrative remedies?
- Must the matter be submitted to arbitration or some other form of alternative dispute resolution before suit can be filed?

Even a beautifully written, compelling complaint won't meet your primary purpose if you don't meet pre-suit requirements. Carefully interview the client, thoroughly research the procedural and substantive law, and consult a practice guide or an experienced practitioner.

IV. COMPONENTS OF A COMPLAINT

If your primary goal is to write a complaint that will survive a motion to dismiss, you must make sure your complaint meets the requirements for your jurisdiction. We'll review typical components required in a complaint here, but, obviously, jurisdictions vary. Always check the applicable rules of civil procedure and local rules to make sure your complaint complies.

A. Caption

At the top of the complaint, you will have a case caption — also called a case "style." This will include the parties and their role (plaintiff or defendant), the court in which the case is filed, and a place for the court clerk to write the case number. (For all subsequent pleadings, you will include the case number instead of leaving a blank for it.) The exact formatting of the caption varies, so it is best to look at local examples before formatting your caption. The following is a typical case caption.

United States District Court
For the Western District of Texas
Austin Division

James Norquist,	)	
Plaintiff	)	**Civil Action No.** _____
	)	
v.	)	
	)	
Alcorn, Inc.,	)	
Defendant	)	

Plaintiff's Original Complaint

B. Title

This, too, can vary by jurisdiction. You are probably filing "Plaintiff's Original Complaint," but you may be filing "Plaintiff's Original Petition," or, later in the case, an amended or supplemental complaint or petition.

After the title you will begin the text of your complaint. Each paragraph should be numbered. Use headings to label each section. For lengthy complaints, full-sentence headings will help guide the reader through the statement of facts.

C. Parties

The parties are typically identified in a fairly generic fashion, such as "Plaintiff James Norquist is an individual residing in Travis County, Texas." Residences are listed to support jurisdiction and venue requirements. Be sure to list service-of-process information for the defendant, including the identity of the registered agent for corporate defendants.

Your identification of the parties does not, however, have to strip their existence down to a mere residence. You can add descriptive details.[1] For example, if the plaintiff is a local mom-and-pop grocery store that has been open on Main Street for 57 years and the defendant is a multinational corporation with distributors in 32 states, you can say that. If you do add descriptions, have a reason for them. Does it make your client more sympathetic or credible in the reader's eyes? Or is it a distracting detail that looks heavy handed?

Writing Tip — Use of Articles

It's an accepted convention of litigation writing to omit the article "the" before *plaintiff*, *defendant*, and other party designations like *petitioner*, *respondent*, and *movant*. These words are often treated like proper nouns, even if they aren't capitalized. Bryan A. Garner, *A Dictionary of Modern Legal Usage* 76–77 (2d ed., Oxford U. Press 1995). Most law students and lawyers are accustomed to the convention and don't even notice it.

But we recommend against extending the convention to other designations like *buyer*, *seller*, *deponent*, *victim*, and the like. You can end up with a litigation document that sounds like a police report. Anne Enquist & Laurel Currie Oates, *Just Writing: Grammar, Punctuation, and Style for the Legal Writer* 134 (3d ed., Aspen Publishers 2009). For example, "Defendant steered the vehicle toward victim."

Use of the article "the" makes the writing sound more like standard English. But whatever convention you choose, be consistent. Garner, *A Dictionary of Modern Legal Usage* at 77. Don't switch back and forth from "plaintiff" to "the plaintiff" when referring to the same party.

D. Basis for Jurisdiction and Venue

The requirements for jurisdiction and venue statements vary by court. In federal court, you'll need to identify the basis for federal jurisdiction over your suit (either federal question or diversity jurisdiction and an appropriate amount in controversy). In a state court of limited jurisdiction, you may also need to identify why your suit is in the proper court. A state court of general jurisdiction may not require a statement of the basis for jurisdiction over the case. Also, consider whether you need to identify the basis for personal jurisdiction over the defendant. Rules also vary regarding whether you are required to state the basis for venue.

---

1. *See* Elizabeth Fajans & Mary R. Falk, *Untold Stories: Restoring Narrative to Pleading Practice*, 15 Leg. Writing 3, 30–37 (2009) (discussing character development as one narrative technique to use in complaint drafting).

Here's an example of a jurisdiction and venue section for a federal complaint.

Jurisdiction and Venue

4. This court has federal-question jurisdiction over this suit under 28 U.S.C. § 1331 because this action arises under federal law, specifically the Americans with Disabilities Act of 1991.

5. This court has personal jurisdiction over Apple Tree Foods because Apple Tree Foods is incorporated in Jefferson and regularly conducts business in Jefferson. The acts creating the cause of action asserted in this lawsuit occurred in Jefferson.

6. Venue is proper in this district under 28 U.S.C. § 1391(b) and (c) because a substantial part of the events giving rise to the claim occurred in this district and because Apple Tree Foods is subject to personal jurisdiction in this district.

If you are filing in state court and want to keep your suit there, you'll also need to avoid including a basis for removal.

E. Factual Allegations

While the rules typically don't require factual allegations to be pled separately from the causes of action, most complaints include a separate section of factual allegations, setting forth the story of the case. Factual allegations can vary greatly along a continuum of specificity. The facts could be as general as this: "The parties entered into an agreement for the sale of widgets. The defendant failed to provide the widgets. The plaintiff suffered damages." Or they could be set forth in a detailed, multi-page account. As discussed below, strategic considerations will control which end of the specificity continuum your complaint approaches.

The following factual allegations fall along the middle of the spectrum.

Facts

7. Chef Luna owns and operates a Mexican-food restaurant in Madison City, Jefferson. Chef Luna opened the restaurant, Luna Azul, in 1998. Luna Azul is a sole proprietorship. Although it took time for the restaurant to gain a following, it began to thrive and earned a profit every month from November 1999 to February 2010.

8. Casa Rita also serves Mexican food in Madison City, Jefferson. Casa Rita is managed by Kim Jackson.

9. Jackson established a Twitter account in 2009. The name on the Twitter account is @JacksonRita.

10. Jackson uses the @JacksonRita account to advertise drink specials for Casa Rita. She also publicizes bands appearing at Casa Rita through the account.

11. Many Mexican food aficionados in Madison City subscribe to the @JacksonRita Twitter account.

12. On February 11, 2010, Jackson sent a message through the @JacksonRita Twitter account stating, "Health department's taking over Chef Luna's kitchen. While he's shut down, margaritas are half price at Casa Rita!"

13. Luna Azul was inspected by the Madison City Health Department on February 11, 2010, but the Health Department did not take over the restaurant. Luna Azul stayed open during the inspection and has remained open during regular business hours since that time.

14. Luna Azul's business has declined by half since Jackson sent the message through Twitter.

15. Casa Rita continued its half-price margarita special for three months after Jackson's announcement via Twitter.

16. Former customers of Luna Azul have told Chef Luna they believed his restaurant was closed after receiving Jackson's message.

F. Causes of Action

After the factual allegations, a complaint typically lists the causes of action the plaintiff is asserting. Together, the factual allegations and causes of action should provide "a short and plain statement of the claim showing that the pleader is entitled to relief." Fed. R. Civ. P. 8(a)(2). (State rules about the specificity required in a complaint vary.) Although the federal rule has contained the same language for years, its interpretation is currently in transition. In the past, courts relied upon the interpretation of Rule 8 from *Conley v. Gibson*: "[A] complaint should not be dismissed for failure to state a claim unless it appears beyond doubt that the plaintiff can prove no set of facts in support of his claim which would entitle him to relief."[2] But in 2007, the Supreme Court in *Bell Atlantic v. Twombly* declared that the standard from *Conley* had "earned its retirement."[3] Instead, *Twombly* requires the plaintiff to plead "enough facts to state a claim to relief that is plausible on its face."[4] The complaint in *Twombly* had to be dismissed because the plaintiffs' allegations had "not nudged their claims across the line from conceivable to plausible."[5] Thus, plaintiffs can now expect their federal court complaints to be evaluated against this plausibility standard. You'll have to research the substantive law for your causes of action to make sure your complaint sets forth a plausible claim. Also, make sure your substantive claims are not governed by a heightened pleading standard, such as those contained in Federal Rule of Civil Procedure 9 for fraud or mistake.

---

2. *Conley v. Gibson*, 355 U.S. 41, 45–46 (1957).
3. *Bell Atlantic v. Twombly*, 550 U.S. 544, 563 (2007).
4. *Id.* at 570.
5. *Id.*

Complaints typically incorporate the factual allegations into the pleading of the causes of action they support. For example, a cause of action based on the factual allegations above might be alleged like this:

Libel Claim

17. Paragraphs 7 through 16 are incorporated in this claim.

18. Casa Rita libeled Chef Luna. Through its manager, Jackson, Casa Rita published a false statement about Chef Luna. This statement was defamatory toward Chef Luna. Casa Rita made the statement knowing that it was false. The statement caused Chef Luna harm by decreasing the amount of business his restaurant receives.

G. Prayer (Also Called "Relief Sought")

The complaint should close with a statement of the relief you are seeking. This should list the types of damages sought. Unless your rules require otherwise, avoid pleading for a specific dollar amount of damages. Little good can come of pinning your client down to a specific amount. Plead too low and you have capped your client's recovery. Plead too high and the client looks greedy. If you are seeking other relief, such as an injunction, specify exactly what you are asking the court to order. Finally, because courts have found that a general prayer for "such other relief to which plaintiff may show itself justly entitled" can support the award of relief you haven't specified, this catchall is typically included in the prayer.

H. Signature Line

The pleading should end with a signature line with counsel's name, bar number, firm, address, e-mail address, telephone number, and fax number.

V. OTHER REQUIREMENTS WHEN FILING A COMPLAINT

In addition to including the typical components of a complaint, you will need to check the rules for other requirements. For example, do you need a Civil Action Cover Sheet? Should your jury demand accompany or be included in your complaint? Is your pleading required to be verified? Do local rules require counsel's name to appear on the first page? Are page numbers and line numbers required to be in a certain format? Does the pleading need to be hole-punched? How many copies do you need to submit? And don't forget the filing fee.

VI. STRATEGIC CONSIDERATIONS FOR COMPLAINTS

Although the minimum requirements for a complaint tell us what you must do to meet your primary purpose — successfully pleading a viable claim — they don't address how to accomplish your other possible purposes or how to reach your secondary audience members. While a dry, sketchy complaint might meet the minimum requirements, you must take other strategic considerations into account in deciding whether to flesh out the complaint with a more detailed story.[6]

A. Encouraging an Early Settlement Offer

You may hope that your lawsuit ends not with a judgment — which could be years down the road — but with a settlement check in hand soon. Should this affect how you draft your complaint?

There are two schools of thought on this question. Some lawyers believe that the best way to "scare the defendant into settling" is to plead with great specificity. The idea is that a detailed, compelling complaint will cause the defendant to realize the validity of the claim, or at least the risk that it presents. A defendant who hasn't taken a claim seriously may be impressed by the pleading of specific facts that demonstrate liability. As Steven Stark says in *Writing to Win*, the goal here is to provoke the reaction, "They know *that*?"[7] Specific pleadings may also provide fodder to a defendant's lawyer who is struggling to get the client to appreciate the gravity of the claim.

But other lawyers believe that the best way to settle a case is to get ready to try it. Nothing should be done in the name of settlement that jeopardizes the ability to try the case. And detailed, specific pleadings may do just that. Once a pleading has spelled out the details, the case is harmed if the facts don't unfold exactly as pled. While some suggest that this danger can be avoided with adequate pre-litigation research, this is a bit naive. Recollections change over time; newly uncovered documents cast events in a different light; discovery reveals new facts. Tying your client down to a detailed complaint can leave that client hamstrung at trial. In addition, you may not want to "tip your hand," revealing to the defendant everything you know from the beginning. Instead of "they know *that*?" on day one, you may be hoping for "I had no idea they knew that!" well into the litigation.

Given these two possible approaches, what is the complaint drafter to do? You'll need to consider your own situation. Ask yourself

- How much contact have you had with the defendant? Have you already communicated the gravity of the situation through phone calls, e-mails, or letters?

---

6. For example, in an article advocating that complaint drafters use "traditional narrative techniques" to "enhance all complaints," Elizabeth Fajans and Mary R. Falk acknowledge that the audiences and purposes of a complaint are often in conflict, necessitating the "exercise of the attorney's best judgment and craft in telling the tale." Fajans & Falk, *supra* note 1, at 15, 53.

7. Steven D. Stark, *Writing to Win: The Legal Writer* 171 (Doubleday 1999).

- Is your claim being taken seriously? What benefit will you gain from educating the defendant with a detailed, specific complaint?
- Do you want to be wedded to the details you are considering pleading?
- Can you include your impressive details in the demand letter but avoid judicial admissions or contradictory pleadings by omitting them from the complaint?

The desire for an early settlement may counsel in favor of some specificity in your pleadings, but consider whether you can communicate with the defendant in some other way, reserving for your pleadings only the statements necessary to state your plausible claim.

B. Persuading the Judge That You Have a Strong Case

The desire to impress your most obvious audience member — the judge — with the seriousness of your case may lead you to plead more than the bare minimum necessary to state a viable claim. Here, too, Stark advocates for detail, saying "Why waste the opening shot by firing a blank?"[8]

But before you start firing, consider who you are firing at. As noted above, some judges will read new complaints filed in their court, while others won't look at a case until action is required. (And even then, that action might not include reading the complaint.) If you know the habits of the judge of your court, you can make an informed decision about whether adding detail to impress the judge is warranted.

Before you can know the judge's habits, though, you must first know who the judge is. In a district or division with multiple judges, the case is likely to be randomly assigned to a judge — *after* you file your complaint. So you won't be able to tailor your complaint to your unknown judge's reading habits. And in a court with a central docket system, the case may be assigned to a different judge for each hearing, meaning that no pleading can be tailored to your audience, and no judge may ever become familiar with the full story of your case.

If you know who your judge will be and that the judge will read the complaint and look upon it more favorably if it tells a compelling story, consider fleshing out your complaint with factual allegations likely to garner support. If you know the judge has a law clerk who will read the complaint, consider whether you can educate the clerk with your complaint. Otherwise, consider holding your fire, stating your plausible claim but saving the storytelling for a document where it will serve a specific purpose.

---

8. *Id.* at 170.

Writing Tip — Naming Parties

Whether in a complaint or other litigation documents, you'll see opening paragraphs that define terms and create short forms like this:

> Plaintiffs Roger T. Howard (hereinafter "Howard") and Leticia Howard (hereinafter "Leticia" and, together with Howard, the "Plaintiffs" or "Howards") bring this action against Austin National Bank (hereinafter "ANB") and Farm Enterprises Service Company (hereinafter "FESCO") for injunctive relief under the Texas Seed Arbitration Act (hereinafter "TSAA").

Of course, in litigation writing, you may need to create and use shortened forms for names and parties, and you'll often need to define those for your readers. But be wise in the way you create and use defined names and terms. "[A]ttorneys may over define, painstakingly (and painfully) shortening every label on the landscape. Such a practice invites ridicule, especially after six or seven names have been defined, names that could never be confused with any others anyway." Karen Larsen, *The Miss Grammar Guidebook* 42 (Or. St. B. 1994).

Try to avoid cluttering up your opening paragraph with a half-dozen defined terms. It's distracting and tedious. Think carefully about whether you need to define the term at all (more on this below). If you do, consider defining later, not in the opening paragraph.

Don't use archaic phrases like "hereinafter" or "hereafter referred to as" to create defined terms.

Don't create a defined term with alternatives, like this: ("Plaintiffs" or "Howards"). You are telling the reader, "I won't be consistent."

Don't create a defined term and never use it again.

You may not need to define terms at all. Specifically:

- If there is only one person with the surname Howard in the document, it is appropriate to give the full name on first reference and shorten to Howard on later references without defining it.
- If there are multiple Howards in the document, give full names on first reference and use first names on later references without defining them.
- If you are shortening a company name to an immediately recognizable alternative, no definition is needed. Burlington Northern & Santa Fe Railway Co. can be shortened on later reference to Burlington Northern without definition. Of course, it's different if there are multiple Burlington Northern entities in the document.
- If there is only one statutory act in the document, give its full name on first reference and shorten it to the "Act" in later references.
- If there are multiple statutory acts referred to by popular name in the document, you can shorten the popular name to something readable and pronounceable, like Seed Act or Seed Arbitration Act, without definition.

One other tip: try to avoid excessive use of acronyms and initials. You don't want an "alphabet soup" flavor to your writing:

In an attempt to control the CRAs, the SEC limits entry into the ratings market through the NRSRO designation. CRAs must obtain NRSRO designation in order to have clout in the market.

Here are some other useful tips:

- Don't invent your own initials. Use well-recognized initials (NCAA, CBS, etc.); otherwise, use words.
- Don't invent acronyms. Use well-recognized acronyms (CERCLA, ERISA, etc.); otherwise, use words.
- Whenever possible, use words, not initials or acronyms. The space and effort you are saving yourself with initials and acronyms can impair the readability of your document.

C. Seeking Favorable Media Attention

Sometimes your client seeks relief a court can't order. Maybe your client wants the public to know that it is cracking down on infringement of its trademark, for example. Or your client hopes to repair an injured reputation with a libel suit against the defendant. If your client truly seeks only media attention and isn't worried about the ultimate judgment, there's little harm to your case from using the complaint to talk to the media. (The harm to your reputation from misuse of the judicial process is another matter.)

But if your client wants both a win and attention for the case, consider whether you can use another vehicle to talk to the media. Would a detailed press release accompanying your more restrained complaint have the desired effect? A press release would allow you to include two things the media wants that don't belong in your complaint. First, the media will want quotations, which usually aren't appropriate for a complaint. Second, the media will want to know the dollar value you assign to the case. As discussed above, you strategically would rather not tie yourself to a specific dollar amount in the complaint. Rather than altering your complaint-drafting strategy to fit the media's needs, write a complaint you are willing to live with throughout the case and communicate with the media in another way.

D. Satisfying Your Client's Desire to Tell Its Story

The desire to talk to the media is often closely related to another goal of the complaint drafter: satisfying your client. Since a plaintiff, by definition, considers itself aggrieved, your client may want to use the complaint to express its grievances. Most cases settle, so the filing of the complaint may be your client's best chance to have its "day in court." Although the occasional addition of details (directly related to the client's claims, of course) may be reasonable to satisfy the client's need to tell its story, keep the potential, *actual* day in court in mind. If the client favors detail that could harm the case by revealing too much, appearing too petty, or otherwise jeopardizing your strategic goals, counsel the client to streamline the pleading and wait patiently for the appropriate time to say more.

E. Invoking Insurance Coverage

A judgment won't do your client much good if there isn't a deep pocket around to satisfy it. Sometimes that deep pocket will come in the form of insurance coverage. (In this respect the plaintiff's and defendant's interests are aligned: Both want insurance coverage for the case.) If possible, obtain a copy of the defendant's insurance policy before drafting your complaint. Then try to draft the complaint so the claims will be covered. Remember that the coverage determination will likely be made by looking at what is contained within the four corners of the complaint.

F. Meeting or Tolling a Limitations Deadline

If you get your suit filed within the limitations deadline, this purpose of filing the complaint will be met. If you discover additional claims as the case proceeds, you may be able to amend your pleadings and rely on the relation-back doctrine to satisfy the limitations deadline, as long as the additional claims arise from the same transaction or occurrence.

Know at the outset whether you will be able to freely amend your pleadings. In some courts, once a response has been filed, you will have to get the court's permission to amend your pleadings. In other courts, you can amend without permission for an extended period of time, sometimes until near the trial date. Even if you can freely amend, don't take that freedom as a license to do shoddy factual investigation or say things your client might later wish to retract. Your earlier pleading can still provide fodder for cross examination of your client.

G. Other Strategic Considerations

Consider one final potential audience member for your complaint: the jury. While an entire complaint is unlikely to be admitted into evidence or read to the jury, portions of the complaint may be read during cross examination or as judicial admissions. Above all else, this means your complaint better be correct. For example, don't risk a painful cross examination by including in your complaint a detail that your client believes to be true but that may later be contradicted during discovery. It is better to write a brief, accurate complaint that sets forth a plausible claim than to write a compelling, heart-wrenching tale that — in front of the jury — proves to be a smidge less than correct.

Finally, the level of specificity desirable for your complaint will be affected by the rules of your court. Three examples come to mind.

First, if you are in federal court facing a possible motion to dismiss (or in a state court with similar rules), you will need to make sure you have included enough detail to set forth a plausible claim. In contrast, if you are in a state court where the only sanction for a less-than-detailed pleading is an order to re-plead, there's little risk in filing a bare-bones pleading.

Second, if the defendant will be required to make paragraph-by-paragraph admissions or denials in response to your complaint, a detailed pleading can force admissions that may drop some matters out of contention in the case.

Third, if the scope of discovery, especially mandatory disclosures, will be controlled by your pleadings, you may want to plead in as much detail as possible about issues on which you want to be sure to trigger disclosures by the defendant. Thorough knowledge of the rules of civil procedure and local rules will assist you in using your pleadings to your best strategic advantage.

VII. CONCLUSION

The complaint has a varied audience and several potential purposes. While you consider all of those, keep the main job of the complaint — pleading a viable claim — squarely in your sights. Failure to comply with the technical requirements for a complaint could make the first document filed in the case one of your last. For a sample complaint, see Appendix C.

4

ANSWERS

Before you consider the audience and purpose for an answer, you must first decide whether to file an answer at all and whether to file any other documents before you file the answer.

I. PRE-ANSWER POSSIBILITIES

Writing an answer may seem like the logical response to service of a complaint. But before you write — or particularly, file — an answer, you need to consider whether that's the right step.

A complete list of all the steps you might decide to take before or in lieu of filing an answer is best left to a treatise on civil procedure. Still, keep in mind that in some jurisdictions, certain pleadings must be filed in a particular order. If you file an answer before you consider the alternatives, you could waive your client's right to challenge certain aspects of the litigation. These things have to be done in the proper order, and the rules of civil procedure for your jurisdiction will control when and in what order you must file documents in the case.

For example, before you file an answer for the defendant, consider whether any of these issues pertain to your case:

- **Personal jurisdiction:** If you want to challenge the court's jurisdiction, that challenge likely needs to be filed before an answer.
- **Subject-matter jurisdiction:** Should you challenge the court's jurisdiction to hear the case?
- **Venue:** If the case is filed in the wrong venue, a motion to transfer venue may need to be filed before the answer.
- **Forum non conveniens:** Even if the venue is proper, if another court would also have jurisdiction and would be a more appropriate forum, you may need to challenge the convenience of the venue.

- **Sufficiency of the service of process:** If the defendant wasn't properly served, a challenge likely needs to precede the answer.
- **Sufficiency of the pleading:** If the pleading fails to state a claim or suffers from other inadequacies, you may need to move to dismiss on that basis or otherwise seek an amendment of the pleadings.
- **Removal:** If the case was filed in state court but a federal court would have jurisdiction and you consider it a preferable forum, consider whether you should remove the case to federal court.
- **Arbitration:** If the case is subject to arbitration, you may need to move to abate the case while arbitration proceeds.
- **Offer to settle:** If you make an early offer to settle that ultimately exceeds the judgment in the case, you may be able to shift some costs and attorneys' fees to the plaintiff.
- **Insurance:** Make sure the defendant has notified its insurance carrier, which may decide to provide the defendant's defense.

II. AUDIENCE

In theory, most audience members for the complaint are also audience members for the answer. So the answer might be read by the judge, the judge's clerk, jurors, the plaintiff, the plaintiff's attorney, members of the media, your client, and your client's insurer. But answers are notoriously dull. The plaintiff's attorney has to read it, and the judge or judge's staff will read it when necessary as the case progresses, but others who get their hands on it aren't likely to read it cover-to-cover.

III. PURPOSE

If the purpose of a complaint is to get a claim on file against the defendant, the purpose of an answer is to keep that claim from resulting in a judgment against the defendant. So the answer's job is to keep alive everything the defendant has to say about the plaintiff's claims. As we've seen, some of the defendant's challenges to the plaintiff's case may be advanced through motions or other documents filed before or with the answer. The challenges that are filed with the answer will usually consist of denials of the plaintiff's allegations or affirmative defenses that would defeat the plaintiff's claims.

IV. COMPONENTS OF AN ANSWER

Again, jurisdictions vary, but here are the typical components of an answer.

A. Caption

The case caption will be the same as the caption on the complaint. If the list of parties is long, the caption can list just the first party on each side and refer generally to the other parties. The blank for the cause number should now be filled in.

B. Title

Check the rules to see if a title is specified for the answer. Is it just "Defendant ABC Corporation's Answer"? Or is it "Defendant ABC Corporation's Original Answer"? These are fine points, but complying carefully with the rules enhances and maintains your credibility. Whatever the rules require, include the client's name in the title so readers can easily identify which defendant's answer this is.

C. Admissions and Denials

After the title, a typical answer will proceed through the numbered paragraphs in the complaint, admitting or denying each. (Under the Federal Rules of Civil Procedure, a defendant that lacks information to form a belief about the truth of an allegation can state that, and the statement will have the same effect as a denial.) Thus a typical answer might start like this:

1. Casa Rita denies the allegations in paragraph 1 of the Complaint.
2. Casa Rita admits the allegations in paragraph 2 of the Complaint.
3. Casa Rita has insufficient information to form a belief about the truth of the allegations in paragraph 3 of the Complaint.

The federal rules require a defendant that does not intend to deny all the allegations in a complaint to specify which allegations are admitted and which are denied—but state rules vary. In Texas, for example, a general denial can be made to the plaintiff's entire complaint.

If you deny an allegation, be sure to do so consistently. It makes no sense to deny an allegation in response to one paragraph and then to admit an allegation in a later paragraph that uses the same terminology.

Be careful in making your admissions or denials, and even in stating that you have insufficient information to admit or deny an allegation. Remember, the answer is the client's answer, not the attorney's answer. You must determine what information your client has. This tale, told to first-year Civil Procedure students, may be apocryphal but it bears repeating: A lawyer preparing an answer for an airline defendant in a crash case is said to have stated that the client had "insufficient information to admit or deny" an allegation that a certain mountain was a certain height. Granted, the lawyer preparing the answer might not have known the height of the mountain, but the airline flying planes over it certainly should. Denying knowledge of that information could prove damaging for the airline. It's the defendant's answer — not your answer.

D. Affirmative Defenses

The answer also needs to list any affirmative defenses upon which the defendant relies. An affirmative defense is an independent reason the plaintiff should not recover, even if its allegations are true. So, for example, a defendant might plead assumption of the risk like this:

> 22. Cadena voluntarily participated in the soccer game, knowing that there was a risk of injury from a collision with another player. Therefore, his claim is barred by the assumption of the risk doctrine.

Federal Rule of Civil Procedure 8(c) contains a list of affirmative defenses. The list isn't comprehensive, and other affirmative defenses may apply in your case, but Rule 8(c) is a good place to start in determining what affirmative defenses your client may need to plead.

E. Special Matters

For certain matters, the answer must plead specific facts. In federal court, for example, a denial of the performance of a condition precedent must be made "with particularity." You should check Federal Rule of Civil Procedure 9, other applicable rules, and the governing body of law to determine whether anything in your answer requires a detailed pleading.

F. Prayer

An answer will typically pray that the plaintiff be denied the relief it seeks and that the defendant be awarded costs and any other relief to which it shows itself justly entitled.

G. Signature Line

The answer should contain a signature line, with counsel's name, bar number, firm, address, telephone number, and fax number.

H. Certificate of Service

You're obliged to serve the answer on the plaintiff — typically through its attorney. The certificate of service is your written statement, affirming that you have done so. The certificate of service should specify what document was served, how it was served, and whom it was served upon.

Avoid nonspecific, outdated forms like this:

Certificate of Service

The undersigned hereby certifies that a true and correct copy of the foregoing was served by first-class mail, postage prepaid, upon all counsel of record.

_____
[signature]

[name]

Instead, opt for simpler language and be specific:

Certificate of Service

I, [name], certify that on [date], I served copies of Defendant ABC Corporation's Original Answer on the following by [type of delivery (such as certified U.S. mail)]:

[list name and address of each attorney served]

_____
[signature]

[name]

I. Verification

In some jurisdictions, some matters are required to be denied "under oath." For those matters, the answer needs to include a verification. The verification is a short statement, signed by the client and notarized, that the specific matters that need to be denied under oath are true. For example, a verification might state that the client has read a certain paragraph of the answer, that those matters are within the client's personal knowledge, and that the statements in the paragraph are true.

Writing Tip — Use of Forms

Forms, templates, precedents, or guides — whatever you call them, no lawyer can try a case without relying to some extent on previous documents. Writing everything from scratch would be too time-consuming and expensive. Besides, it makes sense to take advantage of the experience and accumulated wisdom that is often embodied in a form.

But forms have risks, and you need to use your forms wisely. Here are three risks and three recommendations:

1. Risk: Going on Autopilot. A form can foster haste and laziness. Wayne Schiess, *Better Legal Writing* 195 (Wm. S. Hein & Co. 2005). Some lawyers rely too heavily on the form, assuming that all they need to do is change the names and change the dates. Wrong.

- *Recommendation:* Master the content of your forms. Proofread ruthlessly. Triple-check.

Risk: Overconfidence in the Substance. Your colleague has used this form document as a starting place for years, so what could be wrong? Plenty. Laws change, and so do rules of procedure.

- *Recommendation:* Know what you need and what you don't need in the document. No matter the source of the form, there's no substitute for learning, on your own, what the law requires for the document you're preparing.

Risk: Outdated Legalese. Some forms are full of gobbledygook and archaic legalese. Though often harmless, outdated legalese can be confusing and off-putting.

- *Recommendation:* Once you're sure of the substance—so you won't delete required language—you're empowered to cut the legalese: *comes now, hereinafter, wherefore, undersigned, aforementioned,* and the like.

V. STRATEGIC CONSIDERATIONS FOR ANSWERS

Answers are typically rather dry and formulaic: a paragraph-by-paragraph list of admissions or denials, followed by a list of affirmative defenses. Still, you shouldn't draft your answer on autopilot; you'll need to keep some strategic considerations in mind.

A. Preserving Defenses Versus Identifying Issues

Some answers read like form books. The defendant's lawyer has included every defense possible, without appearing to have made any determination whether one or many of the defenses actually apply in this case. For example, an answer that states that a third party "may" have been the cause of the plaintiff's damages sounds like a kitchen-sink approach.

It's understandable that a defendant's lawyers do this. After all, if the purpose of the answer is to keep your client's potential defenses in play, why not list everything possible? That may be a reasonable strategy during discovery, when it's necessary to keep defenses alive. But remember that pleadings should be made in good faith. An answer that lists every conceivable defense may annoy the judge, who might insist that the answer be trimmed so the judge can identify the defenses that are actually at issue in the case.

B. Giving Your Client Its Say

A typical answer — a list of admissions or denials — doesn't help you cast your client in a favorable light. That's because answers don't contain paragraphs of factual allegations and thus aren't read for the story of the case the way that a complaint might be. Still, you might want to give the reader some idea of your client's side of the story. For example, in addition to denying that your client acted negligently, you might want to point out the steps your client took that demonstrate its care. You also might want to plead facts that explain circumstances that otherwise seem suspect.

C. Giving Fair Warning That an Issue Will Be Contested

If a particular allegation in the complaint is one of the elements of the plaintiff's claim, denying that allegation should suffice to contest the element. But you might sometimes have strategic reasons for specifically pointing out the now-denied element.

For example, in a consumer-protection claim, the plaintiff may need to prove he is a consumer — consumer status is one of the elements of the claim. Often, this type of element is straightforward and uncontested. But if you want to contest that element specifically at trial, relying on the general denial of the consumer-protection claim as a specific denial of the plaintiff's status as a consumer may come off as sneaky. So, although denying the plaintiff's claim under the consumer-protection statute should be enough to contest that element, you might choose to plead specifically that the plaintiff is not a consumer to highlight that this typically uncontested element will be contested in this case.

D. Asserting Your Client's Claims

While you are busy thinking about how to defend against the plaintiff's claims, don't forget to consider whether your client has claims against the plaintiff as well. The defendant may be required to assert those counterclaims in the same suit. Even if a counterclaim is not compulsory, strategy or efficiency may counsel in favor of bringing a permissive counterclaim in the same suit.

VI. Conclusion

It's unlikely that anyone will ever finish reading an answer and think, "What a great piece of writing!" Given that your most likely audience member is your opposing counsel, you needn't be too concerned with garnering favorable reviews for your answers. Instead, focus on preserving the defendant's rights by carefully considering (1) whether to file any other challenges before or in lieu of answering, (2) which allegations to admit and which to deny, (3) what affirmative defenses to assert, and (4) whether to assert any counterclaims. For a sample answer, see Appendix D.

5

CLIENT COMMUNICATIONS

Lawyers tend to talk about cases as if they were *our* cases. But they aren't, of course. The cases belong to the clients, and it is the clients' right to be involved in and informed about their cases. Many of your communications with your clients will be spoken, on the phone or in person. Some will be nonverbal — the meaningful glance during the deposition, the hand on the shoulder as the jury heads off to deliberate. Often, though, you'll communicate with your clients in writing.

I. AUDIENCE

No surprises here. The audience for your client communications really is your client. Because your communications with your client will usually be protected by the attorney-client privilege, there shouldn't be much of a secondary audience for most of your client communications.

But knowing that the audience is your client doesn't give us much to go on. In each case, you'll have to consider the specific situation of that client. Is it a teenage mother who is threatened with losing custody of her baby? Is it a Fortune 500 company that will accept your communications through its Harvard-educated in-house counsel? Is it a busy local businessman to whom the case is an annoyance and a distraction? Because every client will be different, you'll need to target each communication to that particular client's needs.

II. PURPOSE

You will usually have one of two purposes when you communicate with your client. The first purpose is to inform the client. The information may be advice for the client. It may be an update on the status of the case. It may be instructions or a warning about the legal ramifications of proposed conduct. The second purpose is to get the client to take some action, and those actions will also vary. You may want the client to gather documents, prepare for a deposition, or pay your bill. As we'll discuss below, the purpose of the communication ought to be stated at the beginning.

III. Forms of Client Communication

The most common forms for written communication with your client are letters and e-mail. Lawyers frequently don't think of a third form — bills — as client communication. But they should.

You might also communicate with your client through a report in a format mandated by the client. Since the client will dictate what the report should contain, we won't discuss reports here, other than to remind you that a report is a client communication and thus should follow the general principles set forth here.

A. Letters

Formal communications with your client should be in the form of a standard, professional letter. The components of such a letter will be discussed below.

B. E-Mail

Because of the speed and ease of e-mail, you will likely use it frequently for less formal communications with your client. Although e-mail is speedy and easy, avoid lapsing into inappropriate informality when communicating with a client. Like the advice to dress a bit more formally than you think a situation requires, it's best to err on the side of being a bit more formal than the e-mail context seems to necessitate. Don't use "smileys" or other emoticons, and abbreviations like "LOL" are inappropriate for professional e-mail. Use standard capitalization, punctuation, and spelling. Edit and proofread your e-mail messages as carefully as you would a letter.

When your client e-mails you, be responsive. Given the volume of e-mail traffic, you might assume you should respond only when you have a definitive answer. But even if you don't have an answer, your client will appreciate knowing that you got the message and are tending to it. Besides, regular, responsive communication with your client will head off a common cause of complaints against lawyers.[1]

---

1. Steven E. Schemenauer, *What We've Got Here . . . Is a Failure . . . to Communicate: A Statistical Analysis of the Most Common Ethical Complaint*, 30 Hamline L. Rev. 629, 632 (2007); *see also* Jeffrey Miiller & Jill Kohn, *The Top Five Reasons Why Clients Leave and How You Can Prevent It*, Practical Lawyer 53, 55 (Apr. 2008) (stating that the number two reason is "lack of response").

Sometimes, you need to think about whether to use e-mail at all. To make good decisions about e-mail use, apply these two guidelines: (1) Don't do anything by e-mail that you would prefer someone do to you in person,[2] and (2) if the e-mail thread requires more than three replies, you should discuss the matter on the telephone.[3]

Once you've decided to use e-mail, follow these tips.

- **Keep your messages short.** Readers are more likely to give up on reading a long e-mail message than on any other type of writing. As one lawyer told us: "Seven pages of single-spaced text become even more oppressive when cut-and-pasted into an e-mail." So keep it short.
- **Begin with a salutation and end with a sign-off.** Beginning with a salutation ("Dear Beth" or even "Beth") and ending with a sign-off ("Sincerely," "Take care," or just "Best") will give your e-mail messages the appropriate level of formality for attorney-client communications.
- **Use the subject line well.** We've all had the experience of receiving a reply to a forwarded e-mail message with the original subject line, which relates to an entirely different subject. Many busy readers use the subject line to help prioritize their e-mail, and you do them a courtesy when you use a clear and accurate subject line.[4]

Why so many cautions about e-mail? The speed of e-mail often causes us to write, reply, or forward too quickly. And its ease often results in a lack of thoughtful scrutiny. E-mail messages are easy to forward, to include in a reply, and, most dangerous of all, to include in a "reply-to-all." That's why, for example, if you are sending an e-mail message to a client, you should assume your client is going to distribute your message to others.

It does happen: "I have had the pleasure of reading the complete confidential advice of my opposing counsel when her client forwarded it on to my client as part of a back-channel negotiation ploy."[5] Of course, clients can repeat what you say, and they can photocopy and give away your written advice. But both of those types of "forwarding" require more effort than forwarding e-mail, which is just one click away.

So think carefully about whether to use e-mail for a particular client communication, and if you do decide to e-mail, slow down and create a professional message.

C. Bills

When lawyers record their time spent on a matter, they typically see "doing their time" as an annoying task to be completed, not a communication with the

2. David Shipley & Will Schwalbe, *Send: The Essential Guide to Email for Office and Home* 51 (Alfred A. Knopf 2007).
3. Gerald Lebovits, *E-Mail Netiquette for Lawyers*, 81 N.Y. S.B. Assn. J. 64, 64 (Nov./Dec. 2009).
4. Wayne Schiess, *E-Mail Like a Lawyer*, 12 Scribes. J. Leg. Writing 151, 154 (2008–2009).
5. Frederick Hertz, *Safe E-mail Practices for Solos*, Tex. Law. 31 (Aug. 26, 2002).

client. But those time entries will be listed on the bill, and the client is opening that bill at the other end.

So a time entry is a piece of litigation writing, just like the others discussed in this book. The audience is the client. Insurance representatives and auditors may also review the bills. If there's a claim for attorneys' fees in the case, the audience may be larger: Your opposing counsel, the judge, and the jurors may see your bills.

The purpose of your bills, of course, is to get paid. You should write with that purpose in mind. Seasoned litigator Mark Herrmann recommends writing what he calls the "self-justifying bill."[6] A self-justifying bill:

- accurately describes the work performed in a meaningful way;
- describes the tasks in a way that helps the reader understand why the work was necessary; and
- breaks tasks down into different, detailed entries that convey the effort expended.[7]

Your bills should communicate value, but keep in mind that the bills could be produced in discovery if attorneys' fees are at issue in the case. Make sure those detailed entries don't reveal too much about the case. You might want to stick with "analyzed defendant's possible responses to amended claim" instead of "researched statute of limitations problem."

Finally, your communication with your client about the effort you've expended on the case will be more accurate and meaningful if you record your time entries on a daily basis. You will recall more precisely what you worked on that day and your entries will be consistent with other lawyers working on the case.

IV. COMPONENTS OF A CLIENT LETTER

The way you format your letters may be entirely up to you, or your law office may have a standard format you are required to use. The general suggestions here are aimed at those who have a choice about formatting letters. There are entire books on the subject of letters, so for detailed guidance, consult one. We recommend Mary A. De Vries, *The Elements of Correspondence* (Macmillan 1994).

---

6. Mark Herrmann, *The Curmudgeon's Guide to Practicing Law* 95 (ABA 2006).
7. *Id.* at 95–96.

A. Letterhead

For professional-looking legal letters, pre-printed letterhead is best. But if you must create your own letterhead, the recommended approach is to center your name (or your organization's name) and address at the top of the page, with a one-inch margin above. *Note:* In informal correspondence, you may put the return address on the right or left margin.

B. Date (with Optional File or Matter Number)

You may place the date on the left margin, the right margin, or in the center. It depends on your overall letter format. Use traditional, American-style date order, and spell out the month, like this:

September 29, 2009

Not these:

9-29-09
09/29/09
Sept. 29, 2009

For convenience in internally keeping track of files and documents, many law offices require letter writers to place the client and matter identifiers after the date.

C. Recipient Block

In standard letter format, the name and address of the recipient is placed four hard-returns below the date (or below the file/matter number, if there is one).

D. Reference Line

In nearly all legal correspondence, you should include a "reference" or "re:" line. A helpful reference line will identify both the case and the subject of this particular letter. The case-identifying information will allow administrative personnel in your office and the recipient's office to file the letter in the correct file. The subject information will allow anyone looking for this particular letter among the dozens (or hundreds) in the case to find it. Thus, your reference line might look like this:

Re: Bryson v. Carrington Display; Deposition of Mike Carrington

E. Salutation

This will consist of "Dear [recipient's name]" followed by a colon. The comma used in personal correspondence isn't appropriate for a professional letter.

F. Body

The body of the letter is, of course, the heart of your client communication. If the letter analyzes a client's legal issue, the content will be somewhat like a legal memo. You will spell out the analysis, weighing strengths and weaknesses, and you'll make a prediction or recommendation if you were asked to do so. A letter analyzing a client's legal issue might look like this:

As you requested, I have researched whether a court is likely to order that all of your ex-husband's visits with your children be supervised. As this letter will explain, I think it is possible that a court will order supervised visitation. But it is also possible that the most a court will order is that Sam not drive with the children in the car. I recommend that we file a motion to modify the visitation orders to require supervised visitation. If the judge won't order supervised visitation at the hearing, we can request the limit on driving as a fall-back position.

I did not find any cases deciding whether a parent's driving under the influence of alcohol could support an order of supervised visitation. But in two cases, parents who took illegal drugs were ordered to have supervised visitation because the parents put the children in danger while their judgment was impaired from their drug use. In one case, *Salinas*, the mother left her infant son alone in a car for more than an hour. In the other case, *Fredericks*, the toddler son wandered into the street while the father was smoking marijuana.

Those cases should be useful in arguing that Sam's visits with the children should be supervised. But as you probably remember from the divorce hearing, parents' rights to raise their children are considered fundamental rights in Jefferson. That means that while the courts will limit those rights when necessary to protect the children, the courts will not do so lightly. For example, in a 2006 case called *Ismay*, the Jefferson Supreme Court said that a father's visits with his children should not be supervised even though the father injured a co-worker in a fight. The court said that because there was no evidence that the father had ever physically harmed his children or put them in danger, court-ordered supervised visitation was not appropriate.

I am hopeful that a court will order that Sam's visits with the children be supervised because by drinking and driving, he could endanger the children. The facts here are a bit different than *Salinas* and *Fredericks*, though. In both of those cases, the children had already been endangered when the court ordered supervised visitation. Here — thank goodness — we aren't aware of anything that Sam has done yet to endanger the children. Still, I will argue to the court that we shouldn't have to wait for something bad to happen to protect the children. Because Sam has already had an accident while driving drunk, we may be able to convince the court that there is enough of a danger to order supervised visitation at this time. Because of the Jefferson Supreme Court's decision in

Ismay, though, it is possible that the court will say that since there is no evidence that Sam has ever put the children in danger, supervised visitation isn't appropriate at this time. In that case, we can argue that, at a minimum, Sam should be prohibited from driving the children anywhere without another adult in the car. I think our chances of getting the court to order at least that much are good.

Not all client letters will contain a legal analysis. Some will just provide the client with information or instructions. No matter the content, you should provide an up-front summary that states the purpose of the letter. Also, remember your role as an advocate for your client. Your tone should be serious but not alarmist.

For formatting, the typical professional letter will be single-spaced with an extra hard return between paragraphs.

G. Sign-Off

The single word "sincerely" is acceptable as a sign-off in professional correspondence.

H. Name and Signature

The usual practice is to place your typed name four hard returns below the sign-off, then sign your name in between. Signing in blue ink will make the original easy to identify.

I. End Matter

Many things can go here: the initials of the author and the typist ("WCS/kb"), a list of documents enclosed ("encl. Motion to Dismiss"), and the name of others who have received copies ("cc: Donald Reese"). Instead of using the still-acceptable but obviously dated *cc* ("carbon copy"), some prefer to use *copy*, or *copy to*, or *xc* ("extra copy") or just *c*.

V. Up-Front Conclusions

Clients are busy. A client who receives a letter or e-mail from a lawyer will immediately want to know two things: Why are you writing me? What do you want me to do? To communicate effectively with your client, answer those questions immediately, even if you are delivering bad news.

Client letters in particular need to be written so that they orient the reader with at least one of these kinds of summaries:

- The conclusion your letter supports (your ultimate advice to a client, for example).
- The result your letter seeks (the steps you need the client to take, for example).
- An overview of what your letter contains (a synopsis or summary, for example).

There are several other names for this idea: a thesis paragraph, an executive summary, a roadmap. It doesn't matter what you call it; what matters is that you do it — in all but the shortest and simplest of letters — for two good reasons.

First, you are not writing a mystery novel, so do not keep the reader in suspense. The conclusion is the most important piece of information in the letter, so get right to the point and put the conclusion up front. Clients will appreciate having the critical information early.

Second, an up-front summary is a sound analytical and persuasive technique. The up-front summary gives the reader context early on, and context is critical in legal writing. If you set up the context right at the beginning of the letter, you are less likely to lose your reader. What's more, when readers know the conclusion ahead of time, they can fit the analysis that follows into the known framework. Readers will be more likely to square your analysis with your conclusion because the conclusion is already in their minds.

On the other hand, saving the conclusion for the end can cause reader frustration: It may force readers to re-read material to understand it because they did not know in advance where the material was heading. It is frustrating to readers to finish a piece and, when they get to the end, find that they came to the wrong conclusion. If you give the conclusion first, you won't cause that kind of reader frustration.

So if your letter offers analysis and advice, state the advice in the first paragraph. Do not make the reader wade through the whole thing to get to the point. And if you're going to state the advice up front, you should probably include a summary of the issue. For example, you might open with a paragraph like this:

> This letter responds to your question about whether your non-competition covenant with Kathleen Arriaga is enforceable. Given my research, I believe a court will enforce the covenant if you file suit against Ms. Arriaga.

Then, after the up-front conclusion, you can move on to the facts and the legal analysis.

Not all client letters will contain legal advice. You might be writing to report something or to request something; if so, state that first. Depending on the level of detail and the complexity of the letter, you may also summarize the gist of your report or request. For example, if you attended a two-day negotiation on behalf of your client, and you have written a five-page report in letter form, you may want to take a full paragraph to say why you are writing and to summarize the main points of your report.

On the other hand, for a shorter letter, a single sentence will often be effective:

- I have several things to request and report regarding the Bryson matter.
- I need your assistance in gathering information to respond to discovery requests from Wilco Corporation.
- This letter outlines the four remaining matters for us to resolve.
  - (1) . . .
  - (2) . . .
  - (3) . . .
  - (4) . . .

The general principle, for all kinds of client letters (other than a one-sentence transmittal letter), is to start with an explicit, direct, and short statement of the purpose of the letter or, where appropriate, an answer to the question asked.

Writing Tip — Beginning a Letter

Traditionally, the first words the client sees in the text of a letter from a lawyer are often stilted and awkward, particularly if the lawyer is attaching or enclosing a document. You will be tempted to use one of the following ubiquitous phrases:

- Enclosed please find . . .
- Attached please find . . .
- Please find enclosed . . .
- Please find attached . . .

Don't. You will sound much more human and less stuffy if you simply say:

- Here is the brief you requested.
- You asked for a copy of the court's order, so I have included it here.
- I have enclosed my fee statement.

Bryan A. Garner, *The Redbook: A Manual on Legal Style* 188 (2d ed., Thomson West 2006). What's more, you would do well to avoid any of the traditional, stuffy openers that show up so often in lawyers' letters, like these:

- Per our conversation of July 16th . . .
- Pursuant to your request . . .
- I am in receipt of your letter of . . .

These openers are hallmarks of a lawyer but, unfortunately, they are not hallmarks of a clear, professional writer. How much better — and more human — legal letters would sound if we were direct and simple:

- Here is the Holmes memo that you requested on July 16th.
- I am writing to report on the deposition of Tara Knowles taken on August 26.

Write in clear and direct manner, and cut the stuffy openers.

VI. Strategic Considerations for Client Communications

Your goal in every communication you send your client will be to communicate clearly and effectively. Your communications with your client will be most effective if you explain the effect of information on the client's case, manage client expectations, keep communications short, use plain English, and respond to client questions.

A. Explain the Effect of Information on the Client's Case

Frequently your client communication will report on what has happened in the client's case. You might be reporting on information obtained from a witness, testimony given in a deposition, or decisions made at a hearing. Remember that your client is not interested only — or even primarily — in the facts you have to report. The client needs to know how those facts affect the client's case.

Let's say, for example, that you've just taken the deposition of a teacher who has been designated as a fact witness in a divorce case in which you are representing the father. In the course of the deposition you learned that the teacher was a high school classmate of your client's wife. The teacher and your client's wife have remained friends over the years and dine together once a month. If you report these facts to your client, he may find it to be mildly interesting gossip, or he may wonder why you are interested in his child's teacher's social life. Your letter needs to explain that because of the relationship between the teacher and your client's wife, the teacher is less likely to be seen as a credible, neutral witness and is more likely to be seen as a friend who is trying to help your client's wife.

Or say you have just emerged from a summary judgment hearing in which the judge granted your summary judgment motion against the plaintiff's claim for deceptive trade practices but denied your summary judgment motion on the breach of contract claim. If you just report that bare legal result, the client will likely understand that there's good news and bad news, but the client might not understand just what that news means. Your letter should go on to explain that the plaintiff will now be unable to obtain treble damages against the client, but that the plaintiff can still pursue claims for damages and attorneys' fees.

Keep in mind that when your client opens your letter, the client wants to know "What does this mean for my case?" Make sure you provide that explanation.

B. Manage Expectations

Providing an explanation of new developments and their impact on the client's case will help you manage client expectations, but more is required. You must divulge the bad news with the good in each communication. Some of the most uncomfortable moments in an attorney-client relationship occur because the lawyer failed to counsel the client regarding realistic expectations. A plaintiff may have overly optimistic notions of the value of the case, or a defendant may believe the lawyer is going to be able to "just make it all go away." If settlement negotiations begin and the lawyer and client have different beliefs in the strengths and weaknesses of the case, it will be very difficult to reach a resolution of the matter. And if the final result is inconsistent with the client's expectations, the lawyer will be on the short list of people the client blames.

To avoid creating a gap between your understanding of your client's likelihood of success and your client's understanding, make sure that each communication provides a fair assessment. So, for example, if you just deposed the plaintiff's expert and you believe you poked some holes in her theory about the flaws in your client's manufacturing process, by all means, say so. But if the expert's testimony will still be admissible at trial, and the jury will ultimately have to decide whether those holes actually mean your client's process was sound, explain that, too.

C. Keep It Short

Some lawyers tend to save up news for the client and deliver it all in one comprehensive letter or report. Unfortunately, the reporting systems used by some clients encourage this practice. The problem with this approach is that when the client receives a lengthy report on a case, there's a lot of information to digest. It is difficult to do that quickly, and most clients are busy. So the long report is likely to be set aside until the client has time to devote to it. That time may never come, or it may only come when the case has hit a snag.

You will communicate more effectively with the client if you send short, individual letters reporting on each development in the case. The client will be able to read and understand the letters as they arrive. An added benefit is that your client will feel confident that you are keeping the client informed. Your client relationship will be smoother if your client is — and feels — informed.

D. Use Plain English

As we mentioned at the beginning of this chapter, you will have to gauge your client's level of sophistication and write with a tone that is understandable for that client. Even a busy in-house lawyer will appreciate a letter that is written in a readable, natural tone. For other clients, you'll have to consider whether additional modifications to your usual writing style are necessary. Two such modifications to consider are explaining or omitting legal terminology and eliminating or shortening citations.

1. Legal Terminology

For the nonlawyer, many legal terms may sound like another language. You know what a "TRO hearing" is, but will your client? And even if you explain that TRO stands for temporary restraining order, will your client know what that means? For each legal term you write in a letter, stop and consider whether your client will know what it means. If not, you should either use an equivalent everyday term or explain the term to the client. For example, if you find yourself using the phrase "common law," you could instead refer to "court decisions." But if you need to talk about a deposition, and your client won't know what that means, an explanation is in order.

Note that we're not talking here about legalisms, like "said" or "hereinafter" or "same." That kind of jargon has no business in any of your client communications, even if your client is a lawyer.

Writing Tip — Diction

By "diction" we mean word choice, and in English we have many words to choose from.

Imagine a continuum of formality in legal writing:

Informal   *Natural, conversational*   *Formal*

We believe that to make your writing readable, vigorous, and persuasive, you should write in a natural, colloquial tone — neither too informal, slangy, or loose, nor hyper-formal or stiff.

In English generally and in legal writing specifically, for any concept you need to express, you have options along this formality continuum. You can choose a more or less formal word or phrase. You can write *help* or *assist* or *provide assistance*; these examples become increasingly formal. You can write *enclosed please find* or *I have enclosed* or *here are*; these examples become increasingly informal.

It is not our place to tell you where to be on the formality continuum, but we have some advice for finding your own place on it.

First, adapt your tone and style to the document and audience. You often do this without thinking — most lawyers write e-mails much more informally than they do court documents, for example. But you may need to consciously move yourself up or down the formality continuum for a letter to opposing counsel, a letter to a nonlawyer client, a trial brief, and so on.

Second, be consistent. Don't mix obvious formality with obvious informality. Two examples:

- A letter that contains formal diction throughout (*prior to* for *before*, *indicate* for *show*, *elect* for *choose*), with the exception of transition words. The letter writer begins many sentences with conjunctions as transitions: *and*, *but*, *yet*, *so*, and *also*. These light transition words might be appropriate, but the incongruous tone is distracting.
- A letter that uses first person (*I*, *me*, *my*), second person (*you*), and contractions — all of which are fine for a letter — but combines them with otherwise formal diction (*utilize* for *use*, *subsequent to* for *after*, *in connection with* for *about*).

Third, as you gain experience and credibility, move your diction toward the informal end of the continuum whenever you can. Express ideas as simply as you can while preserving the substance. Your reward will be readable, engaging prose.

2. Citations

Citations may be perfectly acceptable if your client is a lawyer. That lawyer may want to look up some of those authorities, so the citations are useful. To the nonlawyer, the citations are probably meaningless. The solution may seem to be just to omit the citations, but that's more easily said than done. Your analysis of the enforceability of your client's covenant not to compete may become rather garbled if you start referring to "this case" and "another case" once the citations are eliminated. A solution is to identify cases by their name, the deciding court, and the year. For example, the first reference might state, "One exception arises from a Texas Supreme Court case called *Fitzgerald*, decided in 2000." Later references can mention the case by name.

E. Be Responsive

If a client seeks your legal advice, your obligation is to determine the answer to the question and convey that answer to the client in a meaningful way. Sometimes lawyers will try to avoid answering a client's question because the lawyer will have to convey bad news. Avoidance doesn't work. If the client asks a question, the client probably understands that at least one of the possible answers isn't favorable. Convey your honest answer. But also keep in mind your role as an advocate for your client. Clients don't like always being told by lawyers what they can't do. Work with the client to help the client find another way to accomplish the client's objectives.

Sometimes a lawyer will not answer the question posed because the lawyer will determine, in the lawyer's infinite wisdom, that the question wasn't really the one the client should have asked. You can't possibly know all the intricacies of your client's life or business. There may be good reasons for the client's question. If you think the client has misunderstood the legal scenario, you can politely attempt to redirect the question before you determine the answer. "You asked me whether we could win a summary judgment in this case, but I think we should first consider whether we could have the complaint dismissed for failure to state a claim." If, as you analyze the client's legal problem, you determine that a different inquiry would be more fruitful for the client, check with the client before taking off in a different direction.

VII. Conclusion

When it comes to client communications, the Golden Rule works well. Imagine yourself receiving advice about a matter outside your area of expertise: the engineering flaw that is causing your house to sink to one side, or the surgery needed to repair your anterior cruciate ligament. You wouldn't want the professional to talk down to you, but you would want the professional to explain the matter clearly, use terminology you could understand, and discuss the ramifications of the recommended course of action. Do likewise for your clients. For a sample client letter, see Appendix E.

6

DISCOVERY REQUESTS

"Discovery" means getting information from the parties and witnesses in a case. Perhaps the most visible discovery device is the deposition. Other than a deposition notice (which is usually formulaic), depositions don't require writing. But the most common written discovery devices — interrogatories, requests for production, and requests for admission — can be cost-efficient information-gathering mechanisms and do require writing.

I. AUDIENCE

Your audience here is narrow. Your primary audience member is opposing counsel. That lawyer will scour your discovery requests, looking for loopholes. The other potential audiences are limited. Opposing counsel will likely send the discovery requests to the opposing party, who will be charged with gathering the responsive information. If opposing counsel objects to your discovery requests (or fails to answer them), a judge may read them. But even then the judge is likely to read only the particular requests at issue, not the entire set. So for discovery requests, pleasing your audience is not a concern. Keeping the audience from objecting is.

II. PURPOSE

The purpose of a discovery request is to obtain information. It's that simple. Although cost may impose limits in some cases, usually you are trying to learn everything you can about your opponent's case and everything your opponent knows about yours. You want to learn what witnesses the opponent will call and what they will say, the documents your opponent will use, and the claims your opponent will make. And you want to find all the evidence that will help prove your assertions.

This goal — learning everything you can — may seem to counsel in favor of broad requests. The downside to broad requests, of course, is that they may be objectionable. If the objections are sustained, you'll be left without the information you need. The perfectly drafted discovery request, then, is just broad enough to encompass every bit of information to which you are entitled, and just narrow enough to survive objections.

III. TYPES OF DISCOVERY

To decide which discovery device will work best to elicit the information you need, you must consider the types of discovery available.

A. Disclosures

You may be entitled to certain information just because a lawsuit has been filed. Depending on the jurisdiction, the other party may be required to disclose this information to you without a request. Under the Federal Rules of Civil Procedure, for example, litigants can expect initial disclosures, expert disclosures, and pretrial disclosures to be provided automatically under the timetable outlined in Rule 26. In other jurisdictions, you may need to request the disclosures before they will be made. Texas Rule of Civil Procedure 194, for example, includes the exact language a party can use to request disclosures from the other side.

Although you won't need to worry about the wording of requests for disclosure, you do need to be familiar with what you will be entitled to through the required or routine disclosures in your jurisdiction. Because the number of interrogatories you can submit will be limited, and because you may face other discovery limits, there's no sense in using (or wasting) another form of discovery for something you are automatically entitled to receive through disclosures.

B. Interrogatories

These are questions posed to a party in the case. Rules of civil procedure typically limit the number of interrogatories a party can submit. For example, Federal Rule of Civil Procedure 33(a)(1) allows a party to serve on any other party no more than 25 interrogatories, "including discrete subparts."

C. Requests for Production

Requests for production are typically requests for documents from another party. In this electronic era, "documents" are likely to be electronically stored information, which may or may not have ever been reduced to a hard copy. Although we typically think of documents when we think of requests for production, keep in mind that you can also ask for tangible items or for permission to enter land.

D. Requests for Admission

A request for admission is just that — a request that a party admit something. Rules vary by jurisdiction, but requests for admission are typically not limited to questions of fact. Under Federal Rule of Civil Procedure 36(a), for example, you can ask a party to admit the truth of matters within the scope of discovery that relate to "facts, the application of law to fact, or opinions about either." You can also ask a party to admit the genuineness of any described documents. Thus, requests for admission can be powerful tools in narrowing the contested issues and streamlining a case.

E. Depositions by Oral Examination

Typically just called "depositions," a deposition by oral examination is live testimony, under oath, in response to a lawyer's live questions. Because depositions can be taken of any person, they are effective tools to gain information from nonparties.

F. Depositions by Written Questions

In a deposition by written questions, a lawyer serves written questions to be asked to any person, including nonparties. Lawyers for each party then have a chance to submit their own cross-questions for the witness. A court reporter then takes the deponent's testimony in response to the questions, without the lawyers present.

G. Request for a Physical or Mental Examination

If a party's mental or physical condition is at issue in a case, the court can order the party to submit to a mental or physical examination. The order will be made only if a party moves for such an examination and shows good cause why it should be ordered.

IV. COMPONENTS OF A WRITTEN DISCOVERY REQUEST

The rules of your jurisdiction and the type of discovery request you are making will control the specifics, but in general, you can expect a discovery request to contain these components.

A. Caption

The same caption of the case will be at the top of the discovery request, even if the discovery is directed at a nonparty.

B. Title

The title should identify the party serving the discovery request, the discovery type, and the party to whom the discovery is directed. For example:

Defendant ABC Corporation's Interrogatories to Plaintiff Karen Smith

If more than one type of discovery is included in the document, name all the types in the title.

C. Instructions

The request should provide instructions for responding to the request. The instructions typically reiterate the requirements in the rules of civil procedure for responding to the requests. The instructions should also provide a deadline for responding.

D. Definitions

If a term is used several times in a discovery request, a definition of that term can eliminate the need to repeat information. For example, if the case involves a fire at a building, rather than repeating the address of the building in numerous requests, you could use a defined term like this:

The term "Building" in these requests means the real property located at 727 Congress Avenue, Davenport, Jefferson 55402.

E. Interrogatories or Requests

Next, you will state your individual questions or requests. Each should be numbered. Use your interrogatories to ask for specific pieces of information. Interrogatories work well to obtain information that requires the responding party to consult records or multiple sources. For example,

1. Identify each employee in the manufacturing department of McLaughlin Fabrications Co. who has a degree in engineering, stating the employee's name, the university that awarded the degree, and the date the degree was obtained.

Historically, requests for production requested physical documents, but frequently today requests for production pertain to electronic data. Thus, your request for production might look like this:

1. All documents relating to efforts to re-design the ¾" steel beams produced by McLaughlin Fabrications Co. to keep the beams from cracking.

But it might look like this:

> 1. All documents containing the consecutive characters "c-r-a-c-k" or "f-r-a-c-t-u-r" in the same document as the characters "b-e-a-m."

If your case is pending in federal court, you and your opposing counsel can discuss at the Rule 26(f) conference how you will conduct electronic discovery, or you can arrange a conference between your clients' respective computer experts.

Requests for admission are useful for determining what is and what is not contested in the case. So you might submit a request like this:

> 1. Admit that Clark Construction was not negligent in installing the ¾″ beams produced by McLaughlin Fabrications Co.

Be aware that subparts of questions are usually counted as separate questions (although permissible subparts may be listed in the rules of civil procedure). You won't be allowed to ask 25 compound questions that really seek 50 different answers. A typical court order in response to a challenge that a set of interrogatories exceeds the permissible number is to require the responder to answer only the first 25 (or whatever the limit is). So put your most critical items first, in case a dispute arises about what should be counted as a subpart.

F. Signature Line

This should match the signature line in your complaint or answer.

G. Certificate of Service

If you copy a certificate of service from a prior document in the case, update it to specify the discovery being served, how it is being served, and upon whom it is being served.

V. STRATEGIC CONSIDERATIONS FOR DISCOVERY

To best use the variety of discovery devices at your disposal, you'll need to think about what information you want, which discovery devices to use, how to phrase your requests to get what you're looking for, and what timing best suits your strategic goals.

A. Consider What Information You Want

It may seem obvious that your first step in discovery ought to be considering what information you want. Unfortunately, it isn't obvious. Lawyers frequently call up their last set of discovery documents from a similar case, make a few revisions as necessary, and send them off without really thinking about what they are trying to get. Your discovery will be more focused and fruitful if you first consider what information you want to have at your disposal when the case goes to trial. As you write your discovery requests, think about three points during the trial.

First, think about what questions will go to the jury at the end of the trial or what findings of fact you will need from the judge. You'll need to obtain evidence to support answers or findings in your favor. So write discovery requests directed at getting that evidence.

Second, picture your closing argument. What do you want to be able to say? Of course you'll address the verdict you hope to get, but you'll also want to make the factfinder *want* to decide in your client's favor. So conduct discovery that will allow you to explain motives or create sympathy. Did the plaintiff go out dancing the night after the accident? Was the defendant corporation facing a huge short-fall that caused it to sidestep some safeguards? Design your discovery so that you'll learn those facts. You don't have to know exactly how you'll get the evidence admitted at trial while you're conducting the discovery. For example, under Federal Rule 26(b)(1), your discovery just has to be relevant and reasonably calculated to lead to the discovery of admissible evidence.

Third, picture your opposing counsel's opening statement. You don't want any surprises there — or at any other point in the trial. So your discovery requests need to ferret out all the complaints the other side has with your client's conduct and all the evidence that will make your client look bad.

B. Use the Best Discovery Device for the Job

Different discovery devices obtain different types of information. Interrogatories are good for gathering specific, detailed information. For example, you may want to know the name and address of all the doctors the plaintiff saw in the last decade. The plaintiff would be unlikely to recall this information on the spot in a deposition but likely can gather the information to respond to an interrogatory. Similarly, if you want to know all the employees who worked on a shift with a particular employee, a written interrogatory is a good way to get that information.

But interrogatories are not suited to getting candid, uncoached responses from witnesses. Lawyers will review — or, more likely, write — interrogatory responses. If you want the party's response without the filter of the party's lawyer, ask the question in a deposition instead.

Depositions are the device that first comes to mind for getting testimony from nonparties. But keep in mind the potential cost savings of using a deposition on written questions instead. Because the lawyers do not attend the deposition on written questions, this can be a cheaper way to obtain straightforward information from nonparties. For example, a custodian of records could be deposed by written questions to prove the authenticity of documents belonging to a nonparty. For complex matters where follow-up or clarifying questions are likely to be needed, a live deposition is better suited to the task.

To eliminate issues from contention in a case, use requests for admission. If the opposing party will have to admit certain matters, send requests for admission to nail down those admissions. This will eliminate the need to gather evidence to prove those matters at trial.

C. Phrase Your Discovery Precisely

Nowhere will your phrasing be scrutinized more than in your discovery requests (unless it is in a contract that someone is trying to escape). You'll want to phrase your requests as broadly and vaguely as possible, so that all of the information you want falls within their scope. But your opposing counsel will read the requests with a magnifying glass, poised to object at the first sign of overbreadth and vagueness. Thus, you must word your requests so that they seek exactly what you are entitled to receive, but not more.

Use simple language in your requests. Avoid words that have two meanings. Wherever possible, take a complex request and break it down into separate requests, each seeking a discrete piece of information. (A limit on the number of permissible requests means you must use care with this approach.)

Defined terms can help simplify the wording of the requests. But be careful when defining a party. Many lawyers define the party as including its agents and lawyers. Doing so, however, may cause your discovery requests to unintentionally seek privileged information. The better approach is to define the party without including the lawyers and then add the lawyers to any specific discovery request in which information is sought from the lawyers. Also, don't define terms you don't use. This may seem obvious, but it happens a lot. For example, a lawyer may copy a definition of the term "accident" from a prior set of discovery, yet never use the term in this set. It is a sign — to your client in particular — of sloppy drafting.

The best way to become adept at drafting discovery requests may be to defend your requests at a hearing. Stand before a judge and justify why the language you used really means what you say it means (and doesn't contain the ambiguities the other side says it contains). The next time you draft discovery, you'll be the one reading with a magnifying glass, looking for any potential objections, so you can cure them in advance.

Writing Tip — Common Ambiguities

An ambiguous discovery request may provoke resistance, cause delay, and go unanswered.

Here are some known ambiguities and some suggestions for avoiding them.

and/or

This little phrase has caused more than its share of problems and has been litigated more often than you might think. Generally, avoid this:

> the car and/or the truck

Here are two better alternatives:

> the car or the truck or both
> the car or the truck but not both

by, from, until

If you give a deadline or time period that prescribes the beginning or ending point with these prepositions, does the time period include the first and last days?

> the response is due by February 15
> the period from April 11 until May 3

Courts have disagreed. The better practice is to be explicit:

> the response is due on or before February 15
> the period from and including April 11 to and including May 3

within

This preposition can denote a forward-running time period or a backward-running time period. Kenneth A. Adams, *A Manual of Style for Contract Drafting* 188 (2d ed., ABA 2008). So this could mean seven days before or after:

> within seven days of the accident

Better practice is to write with specificity. When you use "within," you usually mean a forward-running time period:

> on or before the seventh day after the accident

modifier before a list

When a modifying word precedes a list, does the modifier apply to the first item on the list or to all items?

> charitable schools and hospitals [*Are the hospitals charitable or only the schools?*]

To fix this ambiguity, you must know what you mean. You have at least three options:

> hospitals and charitable schools
> charitable schools and charitable hospitals
> charitable
> (1) schools, and
> (2) hospitals

modifier after a list
When a modifying word follows a list, does the modifier apply to the last item or to all items?

> schools and hospitals in Travis County

Your options:

> hospitals in Travis County and schools
> schools in Travis County and hospitals in Travis County
> the following, located in Travis County
> (1) schools, and
> (2) hospitals

squinting modifiers
Also called a "two-way modifier," a squinting modifier — usually an adverb — is one that could modify either the word or phrase before it or the word or phrase after, like this:

> A lawyer who is late for court frequently loses the case.

This could be referring to a lawyer who is late for court frequently. Or it could be saying that a lawyer who is late for court will lose the case — frequently. Watch for squinting modifiers and move the modifier to fix the ambiguity.

D. Time Your Discovery Strategically

Lawyers sometimes send out "stock" interrogatories and requests for production at the beginning of the case. This might make sense; you might need some basic information and documents before deposing witnesses. But don't just send out discovery reflexively upon receiving a complaint or an answer. Consider whether that's the best strategy for your case. You may want to get the opposing party's fresh testimony on the case. Answering interrogatories or reviewing documents to produce will cause the party to "go to school" on the case, learning coached answers to your likely inquiries or inventing explanations for suspect documents. If you take the party's deposition before sending out your written discovery, you may get more candid testimony.

Taking a party's deposition before conducting written discovery does have its risks. Unless you show a good reason to reopen the deposition later, you'll lose your opportunity to question the party about discovery answers or produced documents. You may omit lines of inquiry to which the written discovery would have led you.

The best strategy for the timing of your discovery will depend on the circumstances of your case. If the case is likely to be document intensive, you probably need to get those documents produced before deposing the opposing party. If you think the opposing party is likely to refine the facts as discovery develops, an immediate deposition may be best in order to pin down the story. If there are multiple witnesses you can question about the same matters (for example, a corporate president and a chief executive officer who were both involved in the decision making), you might get the best of both worlds: Depose one early on; save the other for a clean-up deposition after you have reviewed the documents in the case.

VI. CONCLUSION

Drafting discovery requests may not seem like fun, but it can resemble a game: For each request your offensive coordinator drafts, their defensive coordinator will have a response. To best serve your client's need to get all relevant, available information, carefully think through your opponent's likely responses to your requests and modify your requests to make them thorough yet unassailable. For sample interrogatories, see Appendix F. For sample requests for production, see Appendix G. For sample requests for admission, see Appendix H.

7

DISCOVERY RESPONSES

You would be hard pressed to find a lawyer who enjoys responding to discovery. Many consider it to be the bane of their existence. But responding to discovery is as important as propounding it, so you should learn how to do it effectively.

I. AUDIENCE

Your audience for discovery responses is the same as the audience for discovery requests. Opposing counsel will read your answers, both to learn the information they contain and to determine whether a motion to compel is necessary. Opposing counsel may send your answers to the opposing party. The judge may read your answers if they are used as evidence or if opposing counsel thinks the answers are inadequate or asserts that they limit the evidence you can submit later. Here, too, the judge is likely to read only the particular requests at issue, so pleasing your audience is still not much of a concern.

II. PURPOSE

From the perspective of the responding party, the main purpose of a discovery response is to provide enough information so that you are not limited in the evidence you are allowed to offer at trial. For example, if you fail to answer a request for admission, the matter will be deemed admitted, and you won't be allowed to offer contradictory evidence later. If you fail to identify a witness, you may be prohibited from calling the witness to testify. If you give an incomplete answer to an interrogatory, you may not be allowed to expand on that answer later. If you fail to produce a responsive document, you may be prohibited from using the document at trial.

Other purposes of discovery responses include satisfying your ethical obligations to provide information to your opponent and preserving any valid objections your client has to any of the discovery requests.

III. COMPONENTS OF A WRITTEN DISCOVERY RESPONSE

Your discovery responses will look a lot like the discovery requests. Indeed, they will often be copied and revised from the same document.

A. Caption

The same caption of the case will be at the top of the discovery response.

B. Title

The title should identify the party serving the discovery response, the discovery to which it is responding, and the name of the party who propounded the discovery. For example:

Plaintiff Karen Smith's Responses to Defendant ABC Corporation's Interrogatories

C. General Objections

Lawyers typically list general objections to all of the discovery requests at the beginning of the responses. But judges hate general objections and direct the parties to object specifically to the objectionable requests. If you do have a legitimate objection that applies to all of the discovery — such as an objection that the discovery was served after the discovery deadline in the case — you can list the objection at the beginning of the document.

D. Responses

List each interrogatory or other discovery request. Under each, state your response. The response may be an objection, an answer, or both. For example, if you object to only part of the discovery request, you may object to that part and respond to the remainder. If you will produce documents in response to a discovery request, you can state that all responsive documents will be produced.

E. Signature Line

This should match the signature line in your complaint or answer.

F. Certificate of Service

If you copy a certificate of service from a prior document in the case, update it to specify the discovery responses being served, how they are being served, and upon whom they are being served.

IV. STRATEGIC CONSIDERATIONS FOR DISCOVERY RESPONSES

There is little to be gained but much to be lost in responding to discovery. Sifting through documents at your client's warehouse may not have been your dream job when you went to law school, but you still need to do it with care.

A. Read Questions Closely and Object with Care

Now it is your turn to scrutinize your opponent's requests, identifying any that are objectionable. There's no need to fight about valid requests; just object briefly when you need to do so to protect your client's interests. Typical objections include:

- the requested information is not relevant;
- the request is not reasonably calculated to lead to the discovery of admissible evidence;
- the request is unreasonably cumulative or duplicative;
- the request is unreasonably burdensome;
- the request is overly broad;
- the information is obtainable from some other source that is more convenient, less burdensome, or less expensive;
- the burden or expense of the proposed discovery outweighs its likely benefit; and
- the request is vague or ambiguous.

Writing Tip — Vagueness and Careful Use of Words

In responding to discovery, a lawyer may object that a discovery request is "vague and ambiguous." The lawyer is probably just being thorough and trying to cover all bases, but those two words have different meanings, and careful writers know the difference.

Ambiguous means susceptible of two different, incompatible meanings. For example, "12:00" is ambiguous because it could mean either noon or midnight. But *vague* means inexact and imprecise. For example, the phrase "reasonable efforts" is vague. Ambiguity is to be avoided, but vagueness has its place in

---

law; many legal standards are described in vague terms: best efforts, good faith, reasonableness, and so on. Our point is that you should know the difference. If the discovery request is capable of two meanings, you can object that it is ambiguous. If it is too inexact or imprecise to allow you to respond, you can object that it is vague.

Knowing the difference between other often-confused words is part of being a careful, professional writer. When you use a word incorrectly, you hurt your credibility. Here are some common word-usage mistakes we see in legal writing.

affect/effect

In their typical and most common uses, *affect* is a verb, meaning to influence; *effect* is a noun, meaning a consequence.

- Your decision does not affect [*influence*] me.
- Your decision has no effect [*consequence*] on me.

But both have another meaning:

- He exhibits a bizarre affect [*demeanor — primarily a psychology term*].
- The students were not able to effect [*bring about*] a change in the curriculum.

There is no good mnemonic device to remember the correct meanings of these words; you just have to memorize them.

ensure/insure

To *ensure* is to see to it that something happens: "Please ensure that the motion is filed." But *insure* means to take a financial risk requiring payment for loss: "Our company cannot insure your home against flood damage." Using "insure" when you mean "ensure" is a common mistake.

forgo/forego

This is surely one of the most common spelling errors in legal writing. Perhaps it's because *forgo*, which means "to do without," just looks odd. But it's right. To *forego* is to go before.

that/which

When your intent is to refer to a single item within a potential category, you need to restrict what you're describing — you need "that" and no comma. *That* is restrictive:

- The lawnmower that is broken is in the garage. [*I have more than one lawnmower, and I need to restrict this sentence to the one that is broken.*]

But if you're writing about one thing, and you want to add some extra or clarifying information about that thing, you need a comma and "which." *Which* is nonrestrictive:

- The lawnmower, which is broken, is in the garage. [*I have only one lawnmower, and it is broken.*]

This might help: The difference between "that" with no comma and "which" with a comma is the same as the difference between these two sentences:

- The security guard who attacked me was wearing sunglasses. [*There is more than one security guard, and I'm writing about the one who attacked me — same as the restrictive "that."*]
- The security guard, who attacked me, was wearing sunglasses. [*There is only one security guard and, by the way, he attacked me — same as the nonrestrictive "which" with a comma.*]

Mastering the difference between "that" and "which" can be difficult. If you don't have it down yet, keep studying and default to "that." You'll be right most of the time.

Even if the word mistake you make is an understandable typographical error, you lose the reader for a moment, and you send the subtle message that you don't know or don't care what the correct word is. Watch out for these common typos.

than/then

We all know the difference between these words, but they're easy to mistype. Search your document for them and double-check.

it's/its

Law school graduates should know the difference between *it's*, a contraction for "it is," and *its*, a possessive pronoun. So this mistake is usually a careless error. But if you struggle because "it's" with the apostrophe seems like a possessive, then remember that "its" is like the other possessive pronouns that don't take an apostrophe: hers, his, theirs.

trial/trail

This is a common typing mistake that the spell-checker won't catch. Although it is sometimes funny to see references to the "trail judge" or a "trail lawyer," it's funny only if you're not the author. It's best to do a search for "trail" in every court document you write.

statute/statue

This is another typographical error that the spell-checker won't catch. Proofread carefully.

public/pubic

The granddaddy of them all — a real howler. Don't let yourself be the one to cause the howling.

For further guidance, *see* Bryan A. Garner, *Garner's Modern American Usage* (Oxford U. Press 2009), and H.W. Fowler, *Fowler's Modern English Usage* (Pocket ed., Oxford U. Press 2004).

B. Assert Privilege Correctly

If the requests call for the discovery of privileged information, you must assert the privilege on your client's behalf. Follow the rules for doing so in your jurisdiction. Instead of objecting, you may need to notify the opposing party that you are withholding privileged information and then provide a privilege log that describes the information withheld.

C. Give Fair Answers

Your obligation in responding to discovery is to fairly answer the question asked. If your opponent asks, "Did Karen Smith attend any schools after high school?" a fair answer may be "Yes." If your opponent more astutely asks you to name all the schools the plaintiff attended, you should do so. Remember that if you provide incomplete information, you may be prohibited from providing more complete information later. But you are not required to volunteer information or guess about what your opponent really wants to know.

D. Find and Disclose All Responsive, Nonprivileged Information

Many lawyers turn over to the client the task of locating responsive information and documents. You will certainly need your client to participate in the process, but you need to be actively involved, too. Review with the client all the places that information could be. If your client is a business or other entity, look at its organizational structure. Trace a path through each department that could have responsive information and make sure the appropriate files are searched. Don't assume that your client will find all the relevant documents or information if you just ship the requests off to your client contact.

Why go through all this effort and thoroughness in responding to the opponent's requests? Because it will come back to haunt your case if you don't:

- Your opponent may know that responsive documents exist, and your failure to turn them over could result in sanctions.
- You may need the same evidence to prove part of your case. It won't look good if you can find the information when you need it, but not when the other side requested it.
- Your opponent may suggest that the lack of a document to support an assertion calls the assertion into doubt. ("If they had really done X, they would have a record of it.")
- Your opponent may otherwise comment on your inability to produce a document. ("ABC Company has a record of all these other things, but they haven't turned over a record of this. Why? Did that record contain something bad?")

The last of these raises ethical issues. A lawyer shouldn't suggest foul play where there's no evidence of it. Still, to avoid raising questions about missing documents, search everywhere necessary in your effort to turn over all responsive documents.

Sometimes, despite your best efforts, your client may find more documents or other responsive information after your initial responses are served. Supplement your prior responses as quickly as possible.

V. CONCLUSION

If drafting discovery requests isn't your favorite job, then drafting discovery responses isn't likely to thrill you, either. For motivation, keep your role as your client's advocate in mind. Object if necessary, specifically and accurately, and assert privilege as appropriate under the governing rules. Give fair answers and produce all responsive documents so you don't limit your ability to present your client's case at trial.

8

OPPOSING COUNSEL COMMUNICATIONS

During the course of a case, you'll communicate frequently with your opposing counsel. When the case is active, you may be communicating daily. Most of those communications will be oral — by telephone or in person. But sometimes the communication will be in writing, either by letter or e-mail.

I. AUDIENCE

The audience for a letter to your opposing counsel is, of course, your opposing counsel, right? Not really. The letter will ostensibly be to your opposing counsel. That's who the letter will be addressed to. That's who the letter will seem to talk to. That's who the letter will be sent to. But most of the time, that won't be whom you'll have in mind when you write the letter.

The real audience for most of your letters to opposing counsel will be the judge. If you only needed to communicate with your opposing counsel, it would be much simpler to pick up the phone. If you've gotten to the point of writing a letter, there's probably either a rock in the road or some other need for formality. You will write to your opposing counsel with an eye toward future intervention by the court.

You are also likely to send a copy of the opposing counsel letter to your client. Doing so will keep the client apprised of what is going on in the case and may also help the client appreciate the need for any letter-writing charges that appear on the bill.

II. PURPOSE

The purpose of your letter, then, is not entirely what it might seem. You would expect the purpose of a letter to be to communicate with the person to whom it is addressed. True, on one level you'll be trying to communicate with your opposing counsel. You will be telling your opposing counsel something, asking your opposing counsel something, or asking your opposing counsel to do something.

But while communicating with your opposing counsel is one purpose of your letter, it isn't the only one. In fact, many times it won't even be your primary purpose. Your primary purpose will be to document your communication. You may be trying to show that you attempted to resolve matters amicably with your opposing counsel before asking the court to intervene. Or you may be trying to show that you attempted to cooperate with your opposing counsel, making court intervention unnecessary. If your cooperation has been successful, you may be documenting an agreement you have reached with your opposing counsel.

Thus, while letters to opposing counsel may appear to be close in form to client letters, they actually have a lot in common with affidavits. Both are drafted as potential exhibits to motions.

III. FORMS OF OPPOSING COUNSEL COMMUNICATION

Your written communication with your opposing counsel will likely take one of two forms: e-mail or letters.

A. E-Mail

Because of the speed of e-mail, many lawyers use it these days to communicate with opposing counsel. Although this can be an efficient way to transmit information or send documents electronically, don't let the ease of e-mail trick you into sending messages with inappropriate tone or content. Remember: Your e-mail message could end up attached as an exhibit to a motion or a response, so always keep the "Exhibit A" stamp in mind when sending an e-mail to opposing counsel.

On the job, and particularly when you're working on a lawsuit, every e-mail message you send says something about you and your professionalism. Opposing counsel will judge you, at least partly, by your e-mail. Here are some suggestions to make your e-mail more effective.

- **Pause before you click "send."** Think carefully about the content of the message you're about to send. Ask yourself how your client would react to this message. Are you accomplishing anything constructive?[1] What you write in an e-mail message becomes part of an essentially permanent, searchable record. A person-to-person phone call usually does not.[2]

- **Watch your tone as well as your content.** We should all know better than to thoughtlessly escalate the hostility of a legal matter by using a caustic tone. Yet e-mail almost tends to encourage hot-headed exchanges. We agree with Judge Gerald Lebovits of New York: "E-mail is an imperfect way to resolve differences. Unlike oral communication, e-mail provides no tone or inflection. . . . If communication leads to confrontation, end the dialogue and, if appropriate, agree to speak by telephone or in person."[3]
- **Double-check the "To:" line.** Another pitfall of e-mail is sending a message to the wrong person. Be sure the correct address is listed. The "auto-complete" function of e-mail programs makes it quite easy to send the strategy letter intended for client Bill Jenkins to opposing counsel Bill Jefferson instead. One commentator suggests filling in the "To:" line only after the message is ready to send.[4]
- **Put the question or point up front.** If you are asking a question in the message, ask it first. If the reader needs background to understand the question, ask the question and then give the background. Frankly, an up-front question is more likely to be answered than a question in the middle or at the end of an e-mail message. Likewise, if you are making a point, make it first; then give the support.

B. Letters

The traditional format for communication with your opposing counsel has generally been a business letter. Certain types of opposing counsel communication, such as those intended to form agreements between lawyers and those intended as future exhibits, are best suited to that traditional form.

IV. COMPONENTS OF AN OPPOSING COUNSEL LETTER

A letter to your opposing counsel should have all the components of a business letter. It should be written on the stationery letterhead of your firm or employer. The recipient block should contain your opposing counsel's name,

---

1. Jeffrey Fuisz & Alison King, *Beware the Ease of E-mail*, 26 Legal Times 18, 18 (April 21, 2003).
2. David Shipley & Will Schwalbe, *Send: The Essential Guide to Email for Office and Home* 19, 27 (Alfred A. Knopf 2007).
3. Gerald Lebovits, *E-Mail Netiquette for Lawyers*, 81 N.Y. S.B. Assn. J. 64, 64 (Nov./Dec. 2009) (citing Deborah Bouchoux, *Aspen Handbook for Legal Writers* 141 (2005)).
4. *Id.* at 58 (citing Janice MacAvoy et al., *Think Twice Before You Hit the Send Button! Practical Considerations in the Use of Email*, 54 Prac. Law. 45, 49 (Dec. 2008)).

firm or business name, and mailing address. The letter should be dated and contain a reference line identifying the subject of the letter. The letter should start with a salutation, such as "Dear Mr. Jefferson" or "Dear Bill." (Once you and your opposing counsel have met, either in person or virtually, it is perfectly acceptable to use your opposing counsel's first name. In fact, using the first name is preferable, to avoid stilted formality.) Because this is a business letter, the salutation should be followed by a colon rather than a comma. The body of the letter will follow the salutation. The letter should close with your signature, with your name typed under your signature. If you are copying anyone on the letter or including any enclosures, notations indicating that should be included after the signature line.

Writing Tip — Forms of Address and Sign-Offs

The words you use to address the letter's recipient are the salutation. The universally accepted salutation in professional correspondence is "Dear." Omitting it in a formal letter is unconventional.

Use the recipient's surname (last name) and address men as "Mr." and women as "Ms." unless you know the recipient prefers something else.

Your sign-off (the text above your signature) can range from the highly informal, such as "Best" and "Take care," to the stiffly formal "Very truly yours" and "Yours very sincerely." We recommend the simple "Sincerely."

Your employer may have additional requirements for letters that go out on its letterhead. These might include a reference to the client and matter numbers for filing and recording purposes, a running footer with document-retrieval information, and notations showing the letter's author and typist.

V. STRATEGIC CONSIDERATIONS FOR OPPOSING COUNSEL COMMUNICATIONS

While the format for a letter or e-mail to your opposing counsel is basic, the content and tone of the letter should be governed by several strategic considerations.

A. Provide Context

Although you might know that you're writing a given letter about a previous letter, discovery request, or telephone conversation, the reader might not have the same frame of reference. To make the letter easier for your reader to understand, provide all the necessary context in the letter itself, rather than requiring the reader to pull out other files (or be familiar with spoken communications) to follow along.

Say, for example, that your opposing counsel objected to your request for all of the defendant's documents relating to commissions earned by or paid to any of the defendant's salespeople over the last five years. The objection was that the request was overly broad and unduly burdensome. Your letter could say this:

> I disagree with your objection to our request for production of documents about commissions. We need these documents to determine whether other salespeople suffered the same decrease in referrals that Mr. Bryson experienced. This request shouldn't be too hard to comply with because of the sales-tracking system your client uses.

But a reader is likely to feel a bit lost. What was that request? What objection was made? We get only vague hints and will have to root through the case files to piece the story together. This would be better:

> I disagree with your objection to Bryson's Request for Production No. 4. We need these documents to . . . .

At least now in rooting through the files, the reader knows which document to look for. But why make the reader root at all? Instead, say this:

> This letter addresses your objection to Bryson's Request for Production No. 4. The request asked you to produce:
>
> 4. All documents relating to commissions earned by or paid to any of Carrington Display's salespeople over the last five years.
>
> You objected to the request on the grounds that it was overly broad and unduly burdensome. I believe this objection is unfounded for several reasons. First, ...

Now your reader is prepped to follow your argument about the objection.

You can use a similar approach in other situations. Summarize the letter, conversation, or document that your letter concerns to provide the needed context.

One possible way to provide context is to enclose with the letter copies of any documents at issue. However, we don't recommend this cumbersome solution for two reasons. First, if the letter itself ends up attached as an exhibit to a motion, its enclosures won't be attached (or, if they are, an explanation that these were the attachments will be needed). Second, attaching the copies leaves everyone involved with more documents—exact copies of documents they already have—to keep track of in the case. Instead, just quote the relevant portions of the documents in the letter itself.

B. Include the Necessary Details

If you're writing a letter to your opposing counsel with an eye toward later court intervention, make sure you include all the details you'll want in the letter when you go before the court. If you have a disagreement or a concern about your opposing counsel's conduct, spell out specifically what the issue is, so there can be no doubt later that your position was clear. If you're documenting your opposing counsel's failure to cooperate, spell out your efforts to obtain cooperation. For example, if you're writing the letter because your opposing counsel is not responding to your phone calls, this doesn't make that clear:

> Since we haven't had a chance to discuss this over the phone, I am writing to address your objection to Carrington Display's Interrogatory No. 4.

That could mean your opposing counsel isn't returning your calls, but it could also mean you haven't even left a message. On the other hand, too much documentation can ruin any cooperative tone you are trying to project:

> I have been trying to reach you to discuss your objections to our discovery requests. I called at 9:25 a.m. on Monday, September 12, 2011, and again at 3:30 p.m. on Wednesday, December 14, 2011. I left a detailed message with your assistant both times. You have failed to return my calls.

True, that does document your efforts, but the detailed specifics can come off sounding argumentative and might jeopardize a good working relationship with your opposing counsel. You also risk making the judge think you're a jerk. Instead, opt for a middle approach, along these lines:

> I'd like to see if we can work out an agreement addressing your objections to our discovery requests without needing to get the court involved. Since I've left messages for you twice in the last two weeks and haven't heard back, I thought I'd see if I could address your concerns in writing.

The idea is to document your efforts without sounding off-putting.

Besides documenting your actions, you might be writing the letter to document an agreement you have reached with your opposing counsel. In that case, include any information you would want the court to have to enforce that agreement. So, for example, don't just say this:

> We agree not to oppose your request for an extension of the page limit for your summary judgment motion.

Instead, say this:

> This letter reflects our agreement that we will not oppose your request for an extension of the page limit for your summary judgment motion and that you, in turn, will not object to our request for an extension of the page limit for our response. If this letter accurately states our agreement, please sign and return the letter to me by facsimile today.

Once the signed letter is returned, you'll have an enforceable agreement with clear terms.

If you're writing simply to document a conversation or occurrence for the future, you can recount your version of the events and invite your opposing counsel to make any needed corrections. For example, you might say this:

> If I have misunderstood or misstated what happened, please let me know as soon as possible.

If opposing counsel doesn't contradict your letter but later comes up with a new version of the event, the version in your letter will likely be more credible. Note, though, that you don't have the power to impose agreements through negative notice, such as this: "Unless I hear from you by December 31, I will assume that you have withdrawn your objections to our discovery requests." That language won't create an enforceable agreement.

C. Move the Matter Forward

A letter that merely identifies an issue that needs to be resolved is probably better than no attempt to cooperate with your opposing counsel at all. Still, a letter like this is really just a voicemail message on paper:

> I have tried to reach you by phone to discuss your objections to our discovery, but you haven't returned my calls. Please call me.

Instead, try to find a way to resolve the matter, or at least move the matter toward resolution. Two approaches may be useful to try to move toward resolution. The first approach is to try to convince opposing counsel of the legitimacy of your position. So, for example, you might say something like this:

> You have objected to many of Carrington Display's Requests for Production on the basis that the requests call for the production of documents protected by the attorney-client or work product privileges. However, under Texas Rule of Civil Procedure 193, an assertion of privilege is not grounds for an objection. Instead, the rules call for you to withhold the privileged documents from production and state that you have done so. Upon our request, you must provide us with a log of your privileged documents. Therefore, we ask that you withdraw your privilege objections, withhold the privileged documents, and provide us with a log of the documents withheld.

Notice the reference to the procedural rule. A document that tries to move toward resolution by arguing your position is most likely to be successful if you cite authority that supports your position. Arguing that your position is correct without pointing counsel to authority is unlikely to be successful.

The second approach is to offer a compromise. For example, if opposing counsel has objected that your interrogatory is vague and ambiguous, you can propose a rewritten interrogatory that you would be willing to substitute if the objection were withdrawn. Be careful not to commit yourself to fulfilling your end of the compromise without eliciting a return commitment from your opponent.

It's usually not a good idea to use your letter to propose horse trading ("we'll withdraw this interrogatory if you'll withdraw that one"). Opposing counsel might use your proposed trade to demonstrate that you acknowledge the weakness in your own discovery request.

D. Watch Your Tone

If you think of every letter to opposing counsel as potentially forming an exhibit to a future motion or response, you're more likely to adopt an appropriate tone. After all, if your purpose is to demonstrate that you were calm and cooperative, why adopt a tone that is angry and aggressive? You want to sound completely reasonable in any dispute.

Imagine every letter you write enlarged on an exhibit board and carried into the courthouse. Or imagine the letter as part of a PowerPoint presentation, with one line blown up bigger than the others, "60 Minutes"-style. Imagine a judge, or worse, twelve jurors, passing judgment on you or your client based on that one letter or that one line. If you aren't certain that the language is in your client's best interests, don't write it. If you have any doubt, sit on the letter or e-mail overnight before sending it.

Writing Tip — Tone

Generally, the letters you write in litigation should increase the likelihood of cooperation and resolution, not decrease it. We advocate a tone that is clear and firm but not strident.

Here are three recommendations:

1. Avoid hyperbolic adverbs like *clearly*, *extremely*, and *obviously*; likewise avoid inflammatory adjectives like *absurd*, *blatant*, and *egregious*. Be specific and descriptive and let the facts speak for themselves — don't bolster with exaggerated modifiers.
2. Never engage in name-calling. We are aware of lawyers who, in writing, referred to other lawyers as "an idiot," "a puppet [of another lawyer]," and "despotic." Name-calling hurts only the name-caller, and you can be almost certain your name-calling will find its way into a document that comes before the judge — if not the jury.
3. Never lie, invent facts, or misstate legal authority. You risk more than opposing counsel's cooperation and your own credibility. You risk your license.

We understand the temptation to write a nasty letter to your opponent. Harsh litigation tactics or rude behavior may very well warrant an unpleasant reply. If you need to vent, write the nasty letter . . . and then delete it. Then, write a more measured letter, one that will help your client reach its goal. Send that one instead.

Remember that exaggeration and hyperbole contribute to an inappropriate tone. Calling your opposing counsel's arguments "outrageous" or asserting that the claim is the weakest you have ever seen doesn't advance your client's cause. It just impairs your credibility. A letter that overstates matters defeats the purpose of the letter.

E. Don't Make Yourself Dependent on Your Opposing Counsel

Your opposing counsel has no interest in making matters simpler or easier for you. So don't put yourself in a position to depend on your opposing counsel for anything. If you need your opposing counsel to take action, say so. But have a backup plan, and consider announcing that plan in your letter.

Assume, for example, that your opposing counsel has failed to respond to a request that you be allowed to inspect the premises where the accident occurred. You know you need to document your attempt to work out the matter before filing a motion. But what happens if you send a letter like this?

> Our expert needs to inspect the site where Ms. Kwan was injured. We would like to schedule this inspection for early in May. We expect the inspection to take one hour. Please let me know at your earliest convenience when we can schedule the inspection.

Your idea of "earliest convenience" and your opposing counsel's idea may be entirely different. So what do you do after a week has passed and you haven't gotten a response? Is that long enough to wait before filing a motion? Or do you need to send another letter announcing your intention to file a motion if no response is received? A better approach is to state in your initial letter the deadline and the next step you will take:

> Our expert needs to inspect the site where Ms. Kwan was injured. We would like to schedule this inspection for early in May. We expect the inspection to take one hour. Since I haven't gotten a response to my voicemail messages asking when we can schedule the inspection, I'm writing to ask that you let me know three possible dates in the first two weeks of May when we could conduct the inspection. If I haven't heard from you by April 28, I will file a motion asking the court to order you to open the site to us for inspection.

Now if you file a motion on April 29, opposing counsel won't be surprised, and your conduct will look reasonable. And your letter seeking your opponent's cooperation will be Exhibit A.

VI. CONCLUSION

If you are going to the trouble of writing a letter to your opposing counsel, chances are that you recognize the potential need for court intervention around the corner. In documenting your efforts to resolve matters without bothering the judge, provide context and details, all while maintaining a cooperative and civil tone. For a sample letter to opposing counsel, see Appendix I.

9

MOTIONS

Motions are at the core of modern litigation. Lawyers who would rather be arguing to juries are writing down their arguments instead.[1]

Before we can address the audience and purpose for a motion, we must get our terminology straight.

I. TERMINOLOGY

First, local practice for motions varies. In this book, when we refer to a *motion*, we are referring to a document that asks the court to order something. The motion includes the request and the argument. (Evidence supporting the request is attached to the motion.) That's what *we* mean by "motion," but that may not be what it means in your jurisdiction. In some jurisdictions the motion is only the request, a paragraph asking the court to order relief, but containing no argument. In those jurisdictions, the argument is contained in a brief in support of the motion or in a memorandum of points and authorities. In other jurisdictions what we would consider to be the motion appears in the form of an affidavit signed by the lawyer. So, although you'll likely need to include all the components of motions that we discuss below, those components may appear in one or more documents that may or may not bear the title "motion" in your jurisdiction.

Second, motions themselves vary. Some motions contain simple procedural requests, such as a motion for extension of time. Some motions contain more

---

1. Adam Liptak, *U.S. Suits Multiply, But Fewer Ever Get to Trial, Study Says*, N.Y. Times 11 (Dec. 14, 2003) (reporting study about the decrease in jury trials and increase in written decisions by judges based on papers submitted by the parties).

complex procedural requests, such as a motion to compel or a motion for a protective order. And some motions seek relief that could end (or severely damage) the other side's case, such as a motion for summary judgment or a motion to exclude an expert witness. Generally, the more complex and substantive the motion, the more likely it is to contain all of the components we'll discuss below. For ease of reference, we'll call the smaller motions that seek procedural relief *administrative motions* and the more complex motions *substantive motions*.

II. AUDIENCE

The main audience for a motion is the judge (and the judge's law clerk, perhaps). Your opposing counsel will also read the motion — or scrutinize it, really. You should write with those two audience members in mind. Your motion should give the judge all the information needed to rule in your favor, and it should persuade the judge to do so. Your motion should also anticipate likely responses from your opposing counsel. Granted, your client may read the motion, as may the opposing party, but here your primary focus is the judge.

III. PURPOSE

The purpose of a motion is to persuade the court to order something. That "something" can range from inconsequential to dispositive. You might be asking the court to order that you can have an extra day to serve your discovery responses. You might be asking the court to rule that your client's chief executive officer doesn't have to be deposed. You might be asking the court to exclude the other side's key expert witness from testifying. Or you might be asking the court to dismiss the plaintiff's case.

While the significance of the relief sought can vary, your purpose never should. You should file a motion only to get the relief it seeks — not for other reasons, such as putting your opponent through the cost and labor of responding. If you don't believe there is a good faith basis for granting the relief you seek, don't file the motion.

IV. COMPONENTS OF A MOTION

As we mentioned above, local practices vary significantly regarding which components are included in which document. Local rules may also impose format requirements — particularly length limits — that will control your motion. But usually your motion and its related documents will include the following components.

A. Caption

The same caption as in all court documents prepared in the case should be at the top of the motion.

B. Title

The title should identify who is filing the motion and what relief the motion seeks. If there are only two parties to the case and the relief sought is straightforward, the title will be short. For example, the motion may be, "Defendant's Motion for Summary Judgment." But if there are multiple parties and more nuanced relief is sought, the title may need to be longer to allow the clerk to properly docket the motion. For example, your motion may be, "Defendant ABC Corporation's Motion for Partial Summary Judgment Against Plaintiff Smith's Tortious Interference Claim." Try to keep the title as short as the situation allows.

C. Opening

At the very beginning of your motion, tell the court what this motion concerns. What relief does the motion seek? One way to decide what to put in this opener is this: Often when lawyers approach counsel's table to argue a motion, the judge will ask the lawyer who filed the motion, "Counselor, what are we here on?" The opening sentence or paragraph of your motion should be the answer to that question.[2]

Writing Tip — Up-Front Summaries

Many forms or templates for trial motions contain an opening paragraph that states the parties' names and the title of the motion, like this:

Defendants' Motion for Summary Judgment

> William Adams and ABC Corporation (collectively "Defendants"), file this Defendants' Motion for Summary Judgment against all claims of Rene Selter ("Plaintiff"), in the above-referenced matter and would respectfully show unto the court as follows.

Although this traditional approach is comfortable to many lawyers, we think it is a poor way to begin a motion that is intended to persuade a judge to grant your

---

2. For examples of rewrites of traditional opening paragraphs, *see* Wayne Schiess, *The Bold Synopsis: A Way to Improve Your Motions*, 63 Tex. Bar. J. 1030 (2000); Beverly Ray Burlingame, *On Beginning a Court Paper*, 6 Scribes J. Leg. Writing 160 (1997).

request. Instead of restating the parties' names and the title of the motion, get right to the point and state why you are entitled to the order you seek.

Defendants' Motion for Summary Judgment

> William Adams and ABC Corporation move for summary judgment because they were never the plaintiff's employer under Texas law. In addition, the plaintiff has not exhausted her administrative remedies.

Now the judge knows, quickly and right up front, why you should get what you're asking for. You have not wasted the judge's time with needless preliminaries, and you have used the opening paragraph for persuasion instead of redundancy. *See* Kirsten K. Davis, *Persuasion Through Organization: Roadmap Paragraphs*, Ariz. Law. 26, 27 (Nov. 2004).

D. Introduction or Preliminary Statement

The opening will orient the judge to the relief this particular motion seeks, but the judge will still need some grounding in what this case concerns and how this motion fits into that bigger picture. Your next section, typically labeled "Introduction" or "Preliminary Statement," should provide that orientation. The judge may not have read any other documents in the case, so you'll need to explain (briefly) what the case is about. Then you'll need to explain how the relief sought in the motion relates to the overall case. For example, you might first explain that this is a suit for breach of a covenant not to compete. Then you might explain that the plaintiff sought discovery of customer lists used by the defendant. Then you might explain that this Motion for a Protective Order seeks to protect the defendant's customer lists from discovery.

Here's an example of an introduction for a motion seeking to prevent the defendant's president from being deposed:

Introduction

The plaintiff, Chef Jorge Luna, should not be allowed to depose the president of Festive Foods, Inc. The requirements for taking this apex deposition have not been met. In this libel suit, Chef Luna seeks damages he claims he suffered as a result of a message sent through the Twitter account of the manager of the Madison City location of Casa Rita. Casa Rita contends that the manager, Kim Jackson, was not acting within the course and scope of her employment when she sent the message.

Casa Rita is owned by Festive Foods, Inc., a Delaware corporation that owns more than 150 restaurants. Chef Luna has noticed the deposition of Eduardo Ramirez, the president of Festive Foods, Inc. Because Mr. Ramirez has no unique or superior personal knowledge of facts relevant to this suit and because the plaintiff has not sought to obtain the information through less intrusive means, Casa Rita asks the Court to issue an order prohibiting the plaintiff from taking Mr. Ramirez's deposition.

The opening paragraph and introduction in an administrative motion may be combined with the statement of facts and argument. For example, if you seek an extension of a page limit, your opening paragraph can simply request the extension and state why it is necessary. The entire motion may be contained in that one paragraph.

But for longer motions, don't neglect the opportunity to give the judge the context necessary to understand the motion. Providing that context will allow the judge to understand the significance of the facts that follow.[3]

E. Statement of Facts

Next, in a section labeled "facts" or "statement of facts," you should explain the facts that pertain to your motion. A brief overview of the facts of the case, or a context-setting statement, may be appropriate, but keep the overview short. A sentence or two should suffice. Then focus on the facts that are relevant to your motion. Of course, if you are filing a case-dispositive motion, such as a motion for summary judgment, the facts of the case and the facts pertinent to your motion are the same. But for other motions, the judge may not need to understand much about the case to decide whether to grant the relief you are seeking.

For example, in the motion seeking to prevent the defendant's president from being deposed, the facts relating to the underlying suit will be mentioned only as they relate to the motion:

Facts

Mr. Ramirez is president of Festive Foods, the Delaware corporation that owns Casa Rita. (Aff. Eduardo Ramirez (Sept. 13, 2011), attached as Exhibit A.) In this position, Mr. Ramirez oversees the company's operations. (*Id.*) Festive Foods owns more than 150 restaurants throughout the United States. (*Id.*) Mr. Ramirez's responsibilities include supervising the company's strategic planning, new market development, and budgeting. (*Id.*) Mr. Ramirez has no day-to-day involvement with the management of individual restaurants. (*Id.*)

Mr. Ramirez has not visited the Madison City location of Casa Rita since 2003. (*Id.*) He has never met Kim Jackson, the current manager of Casa Rita's Madison City restaurant. (*Id.*)

In this suit, Chef Luna claims damages because of a message sent through Jackson's Twitter account. (Pl.'s Compl. ¶ 5–9, May 12, 2011.) On September 9,

---

3. Stephen V. Armstrong & Timothy P. Terrell, *Thinking Like a Writer* 15 (3d ed., Practising L. Inst. 2009) (discussing principle of "super-clarity," that "[r]eaders absorb information best if they understand its significance as soon as they see it.").

Chef Luna noticed the deposition of Mr. Ramirez, to take place on September 26, 2011. (Ramirez Depo. Notice (Sept. 9, 2011), attached as Exhibit B.)

Mr. Ramirez has no personal knowledge of any facts relating to this lawsuit. (Ex. A.) Mr. Ramirez is not familiar with Ms. Jackson's responsibilities at Casa Rita and was unaware of the Twitter message until after this suit was filed. (*Id.*)

Use appropriate writing techniques to persuasively tell the story of your motion.[4] The judge may be unfamiliar with your case before reading the motion, so this is your chance to put your client in the most favorable light possible. Avoid characterizations (using adjectives and adverbs) that attempt to force on the judge a particular conclusion. Instead, state facts that will lead the judge to the desired conclusion. As Armstrong and Terrell recommend, consider from whose point of view you tell the story, where you start and end the story, and where you add and omit detail.[5]

Every fact relied upon in the motion must be proved by evidence. A thorough statement of facts will cite that evidence after each fact. (Sometimes local rules require this.) At a minimum, state in the motion what evidence is attached to the motion. For example, your motion might state, "This motion is supported by the affidavit of Jerry Martinez, attached as Exhibit A; excerpts from the deposition of William Adams, attached as Exhibit B; and Plaintiff's Responses to ABC Corporation's Requests for Admission, attached as Exhibit C."

In an administrative motion, the statement of facts may be omitted if the few pertinent facts can be incorporated into the argument.

F. Motion Standard

Next, state the standard that the judge must apply in deciding the motion. For example, if the motion is a motion for summary judgment, your motion standard section might state that the judge should grant the motion "if the pleadings, the discovery and disclosure materials on file, and any affidavits show that there is no genuine issue as to any material fact and that the movant is entitled to judgment as a matter of law."[6] Cite binding authority for the standard.

Many motions refer to this section as the "standard of review" section. But because the motion is up for initial consideration rather than review, "motion standard" more accurately labels the section.[7]

---

4. For discussions of writing techniques you can use, *see* Gregory G. Colomb & Joseph M. Williams, *Shaping Stories: Managing the Appearance of Responsibility*, 6 Persps.: Teaching Leg. Research & Writing 16 (1997); Stephen V. Armstrong & Timothy P. Terrell, *Organizing Facts to Tell Stories*, 9 Persps.: Teaching Leg. Research & Writing 90 (2001).

5. Armstrong & Terrell, *supra* note 4, at 90.

6. Fed. R. Civ. P. 56(c).

7. Mary Beth Beazley, *A Practical Guide to Appellate Advocacy* 21 (3d ed., Aspen Publishers 2006) (distinguishing between appellate standards of review and motions standards).

In administrative motions that present matters within the judge's discretion, the motion standard section is often omitted.

G. Argument and Authorities

The Argument and Authorities section is the centerpiece of the motion. In it, you should prove why your client is entitled to the relief sought.

The length and organization of the Argument and Authorities section will vary depending on complexity of the issues presented. In an administrative motion, you may cite authority showing that the court is empowered to grant the relief sought, explain authority showing that other courts have granted relief in circumstances similar to yours, and then compare that authority to your facts to show why you are entitled to the relief.

In a substantive motion, you should organize your argument around the issues the court will need to decide. First, provide the court with an overview of the law that shows what the issues are. In that overview you can dispose of any issues that are not in dispute in the motion. Then provide a roadmap for the order in which you will address the contested issues.[8]

A roadmap paragraph for a motion for summary judgment might look like this:

> Summary judgment should be granted against Katie Kelley's claim for public disclosure of embarrassing private facts. Under Texas law, the tort of public disclosure of embarrassing private facts has three elements: (1) publicity was given to matters concerning one's personal life, (2) publication would be highly offensive to a reasonable person of ordinary sensibilities, and (3) the matter publicized is not of legitimate public concern. *Star-Telegram, Inc. v. Doe*, 915 S.W.2d 471, 473–74 (Tex. 1995). The summary judgment evidence disproves the second and third elements: Publication of the facts regarding the attack on Ms. Kelley would not be offensive to a reasonable person, and the matter was of legitimate public concern. Therefore, summary judgment is appropriate.

For each contested issue, you should usually follow the organizational structure typically used for legal analysis.[9] First, state your conclusion on the issue, phrased in terms of the case before the court. Then state and explain the governing law. After you have explained the law, apply it to your facts. Explain how the governing law applies to your case or make specific, fact-based comparisons to the precedents to demonstrate why a particular standard is or is not met. Make sure any facts on which you rely in applying the law were included in your

---

8. Darby Dickerson, *Motion Potion: Tips for Magical Memoranda*, 16 No. 1 Prac. Litig. 7, 8 (Jan. 2005).

9. Beazley, *supra* note 7, at 75–76 (identifying the syllogistic formulas typically taught to first-year students as a method for organizing legal analysis, variously labeled IRAC, CREAC, IREAC, and CRuPAC).

Statement of Facts and supported by the evidence attached to your motion. After your application, you may rebut your opponent's best counterarguments, and then re-state your conclusion on that issue. When you are finished addressing each contested issue, show how the conclusions on each issue add up to the overall conclusion that your client is entitled to the relief sought.

In crafting this argument, remember that trial judges are busy. Your argument needs to provide the judge with all the information needed to decide the motion, and you must prove each step necessary to the relief you seek. But don't waste the judge's time belaboring the obvious. If your motion concerns a well-settled rule of law, your conclusion, rule, and rule explanation might be contained in a sentence or two. Conversely, if the key issue in the motion is about what the rule of law is on a particular point, you may need to argue in some depth about what the rule of law is. But then your application section might be quite brief. Expand or collapse the rule, rule explanation, and application sections to provide the judge with the necessary information, but no more.

H. Prayer (Also Called "Relief Sought")

The motion should identify the specific relief sought. Rather than just asking that the motion be granted, preview the language you want to see in the court's order. For example, your prayer in a motion to compel might say:

> Defendant asks that the court grant this motion and order Plaintiff Luna to respond to Interrogatory 4 within ten days of the court's order.

I. Signature Line

This should match the signature line in your complaint or answer.

J. Certificate of Service

If you copy a certificate of service from a prior document in the case, update it to specify the motion being served, how it is being served, and upon whom it is being served.

K. Certificate of Conference

In some jurisdictions, you may be required to certify that you have attempted to resolve the issue without the need for court intervention. This requirement will probably apply only to administrative motions that could be resolved by agreement, not to substantive motions on which agreement could not reasonably be expected.

L. Evidence

Attach evidence to prove each fact upon which your motion relies. The procedural rules don't acknowledge a difference, but in practice the formality differs for administrative motions and substantive motions. For a substantive motion, comply with all the formalities. Any piece of evidence attached to the motion should be "proved up" with an affidavit proving that the document is what it purports to be and is not hearsay. For administrative motions, it is not unusual to see discovery requests or letters between counsel attached to the motion without being proved up (although there's no harm in doing so).

V. Strategic Considerations for Motions

The most important strategic decision you will make with regard to a motion is whether to file one at all. Once you have decided to file, rely only on binding authority if possible, write persuasively without appearing to persuade, and anticipate the response.

A. Decide Carefully Whether to File a Motion

Deciding whether to file a motion will be different for administrative motions and substantive motions. For administrative motions, file only if you must. Judges want lawyers to work out their own administrative matters. They hate "babysitting." Lawyers who fail to work out their administrative matters risk incurring the wrath of the judge. Some judges are quite adept at making both parties (and their lawyers) feel the pain if a judge has to be brought in to resolve administrative matters. Cooperate wherever possible. If you can agree on a matter but still need an order in place (such as an order to protect confidential materials from disclosure), simply agree upon the terms and present the judge with an agreed order. Otherwise, file an administrative motion at your own peril.

For substantive motions, you owe it to your client to assess realistically your chance of getting the motion granted. Even if you have a good faith basis for your motion (and thus won't violate ethical rules by filing it), you still might realize that your chances of getting relief are slim. Drafting a substantive motion and gathering the evidence to support it are expensive undertakings. Don't undertake them lightly.

Some cases are appropriate for substantive motions. These include:

- Cases that will be resolved on a legal issue. For example, if the parties agree on the facts but dispute whether a particular claim or defense exists as a matter of law, a motion for summary judgment is appropriate to seek resolution of the legal issue.
- Cases in which the defendant doesn't have a valid defense. For example, in some suits on a debt, the debtor doesn't have a defense but is just trying to

delay the inevitable. No trial is needed; a summary judgment motion can be used to obtain the judgment.

- Cases in which a partial summary judgment motion can be used to narrow the issues. For example, if the plaintiff has asserted multiple claims but only some present fact issues, a partial summary judgment motion can be used to knock out extraneous claims and possibly bring the parties to the bargaining table on those that remain. But be careful what you ask for. A successful motion for partial summary judgment could result in evidence favorable to your client being excluded at trial because it is no longer relevant to any live issues in the case.

- Cases in which discovery produces case-ending evidence. For example, if the plaintiff filed a fraud claim but then admitted in a deposition that there was no reliance on the allegedly fraudulent statement, you have a good candidate for a motion for summary judgment.

- Cases in which the plaintiff has failed to plead a plausible claim. As discussed in Chapter 3, the United States Supreme Court has been tightening up the requirements for pleading a viable claim. Complaints that would have withstood motions to dismiss under the old standards may now be vulnerable to a motion to dismiss.[10]

- Cases in which your opponent's expert's opinions are not reliable. Because expert testimony is necessary to prove many claims, excluding your opponent's expert from testifying can have a devastating impact on your opponent's case. If your opponent's expert's opinions don't meet the requirements set forth in *Daubert v. Merrell Dow Pharmaceuticals*, file a motion to exclude their testimony.[11]

Keep in mind the uphill battle you face to get a substantive motion granted. The judge won't grant a motion for summary judgment if a material fact issue is presented, even if your ten affidavits contradict your opponent's one. Usually judges can be reversed for granting summary judgments, but not for denying them. Likewise, if the judge denies a motion to exclude an expert, the record will contain the expert's testimony, allowing the appellate court to decide its admissibility based on a full record. If the judge grants a motion to exclude expert testimony, a remand may be necessary because the expert's testimony is not before the appellate court.

Bottom line: Take a clean shot if you have one, but otherwise save your ammunition for trial.

---

10. *See Bell Atlantic Corp. v. Twombly*, 550 U.S. 544, 563 (2007) (deciding that the old often-quoted pleading standard had "earned its retirement"); *see also Ashcroft v. Iqbal*, 129 S. Ct. 1937, 1953 (2009) (noting that *Twombly* "expounded the pleading standard for 'all civil actions'").

11. *See Daubert v. Merrell Dow Pharmaceuticals, Inc.*, 509 U.S. 579 (1993).

B. Rely on Binding Authority if Possible

The trial court is at the bottom of the hierarchy of authority. Its decisions are likely constrained by both an intermediate appellate court and a high court. A state court deciding an issue of federal law will also have United States Supreme Court authority constraining its decision. Because the trial court is at the bottom of the pecking order, it will care most about binding authority. Arguments based on persuasive authority and policy arguments are unlikely to persuade the trial judge except on issues of first impression. If you are trying to preserve an issue for appeal, you may need to cite to persuasive authority or rely on policy arguments. Otherwise, stick to telling the trial court what its bosses have to say on the issue.

Don't make the mistake of tacking persuasive authority on to your citation under the theory that it can't hurt. It can hurt. A judge who sees a string citation to a binding case and to a persuasive one is likely to conclude that the binding case didn't quite support the motion's assertion and so you tacked on the persuasive authority to bolster the support.[12] If the binding authority supports your assertion, cite it and leave it at that.

Writing Tip — Citing Authority

In stating and explaining the governing law, you'll need to cite legal authority. Legal citations are mind-numbingly tedious yet critically important. Both the substance and the form of your legal citations affect your credibility with the judge. Some things to keep in mind:

- Lengthy string citations with no explanation will often annoy judges. Usually you need to cite only one or two cases for a key proposition — enough to show that the proposition is still good law. If you feel you must cite several cases, explain why citation to several cases is helpful.
- Incorrect citation form can hurt your credibility. Generally, judges care mostly that the authority can be found, not that every abbreviation, space, and comma is perfect. But remember that judges have clerks who were recently staffers or editors on law reviews. Incorrect citation form may harm your credibility with these important readers.
- Just as important as correct citation form is consistent citation form. Whatever edition of the citation manual you're using, be consistent in your citation form. Don't mix italics and underlining. Always abbreviate the same words the same way. Make short citation forms consistent.

---

12. Steven D. Stark, *Writing to Win: The Legal Writer* 133 (Doubleday 1999).

C. Write Persuasively Without Appearing to Persuade

A persuasive motion will prove that your client is entitled to the relief sought. Using the law and the evidence, an effective motion should lead the judge to the inevitable conclusion that your relief should be granted. To help the judge decide in your favor, cite authority that creates confidence that granting your relief will not lead to reversal.

In addition to relying on the weight of legal authority, you will also want to write persuasively. Your goal is persuading without seeming to persuade; you don't want to sound strident. A judge is more likely to trust a motion that provides a reliable guide to the conclusion than a motion that pushes too hard. Think teaching, not door-to-door sales.

Entire books have been written about persuasion in legal writing, and we recommend these:

- Michael R. Smith, *Advanced Legal Writing: Theories and Strategies in Persuasive Writing* (2d ed., Aspen Publishers 2008).
- Ross Guberman, *Point Made: How to Write Like the Nation's Top Advocates* (Oxford U. Press 2011).
- Kenneth F. Oettle, *Making Your Point: A Practical Guide to Persuasive Legal Writing* (ALM 2007).

Below, we offer a few of the most important techniques for persuading in a motion.

1. Credibility

If a judge can trust you and what you've written in your motion, you've gone a long way toward persuading that judge. Thus, displaying professional credibility is an important key to persuasion. True, credibility is a trait, not a technique; it's something you show, not something you do. To show you're credible and to earn the judge's trust, remember three key concepts: care, candor, and honesty.

Care. Show the judge that you can be trusted with the small things, and you earn credibility with larger things. Read and follow the local rules, and be sure your motion — and any other court document — complies with them. Use correct citation form and always provide accurate pinpoint citations. The absence of pinpoint citations harms your credibility, and their absence is a particular pet peeve of many judges.[13] And cite the record — please cite the record. A frequent complaint of judges is the omission of record citations.[14] We're aware of multiple

---

13. Terri LeClercq, *Expert Legal Writing* 34 (U. Tex. Press 1995).
14. *State ex rel. Physicians Comm. for Responsible Medicine v. Bd. Trustees of Ohio S. Univ.*, 843 N.E.2d 174, 177 (Ohio 2006).

cases in which lawyers were reprimanded or sanctioned for failing to adequately cite the record.[15]

Candor. Is there a bad fact in your case? Don't hide it; address it. Explain it and put it in context. You'll earn credibility points. Did you find a case that hurts your position? Cite it. Show why it doesn't apply or how it should be distinguished. In some situations, according to Model Rules of Professional Conduct 3.3(a)(3), you may be required to cite adverse authority. But even when you're not required to do so, you should avoid the appearance that you are hiding something. Lawyers who omit unfavorable authority with this "ostrich-like tactic" have been sanctioned or rebuked.[16]

Honesty. Never lie about the facts of your case and never lie about the law. Of course, doing so could violate ethics rules, such as Model Rules of Professional Conduct 3.3(a)(1). But you also damage your credibility. The judge and court staff will likely discover your dishonesty, and even if they don't, opposing counsel is getting paid to find your mistakes. Don't risk it. "Arguably, the most important character trait for legal writers to project to their readers is *truthfulness.*"[17] Our advice goes beyond not lying: Never distort or mischaracterize. "The first time the judge thinks you have played fast and loose, your credibility — and possibly your client's case — will be lost."[18]

2. Story

A compelling story is powerful, and if you can present your client's requested relief as a narrative, you will enhance its persuasiveness. In a live presentation before a jury, trial lawyers often use the story of the case to persuade, and paying more attention to narrative can lead to a more persuasive motion as well.[19]

Naturally, you'll tell your client's story in the facts statement of a motion, but you need not stop there. Return to that story or theme in the argument as well. Even though rule-based analysis or analogies will be key tools for forming your legal arguments, "stories can enhance, rather than conflict with, analytical reasoning and are appropriate decisionmaking tools."[20]

---

15. *Smith v. Emery*, 856 P.2d 1386, 1390 (Nev. 1993) (lawyer sanctioned for filing two briefs that contained no record citations); *Island Harbor Beach Club v. Dept. Nat. Resources*, 471 So. 2d 1380, 1381 (Fla. Dist. App. 1985) (thirteen-page statement of facts contained only seven record citations; brief stricken).

16. Judith D. Fischer, *Pleasing the Court: Writing Ethical and Effective Briefs* 9 (Carolina Academic Press 2005) (citing examples).

17. Michael R. Smith, *Advanced Legal Writing: Theories and Strategies in Persuasive Writing* 126 (2d ed., Aspen Publishers 2008) (emphasis in original).

18. Dickerson, *supra* note 8, at 9.

19. *See* Kenneth D. Chestek, *The Plot Thickens: Appellate Brief as Story*, 14 Leg. Writing: J. Leg. Writing Inst. 127, 131–32 (2008).

20. Steven J. Johansen, *This Is Not the Whole Truth: The Ethics of Telling Stories to Clients*, 38 Ariz. St. L.J. 961, 962 (2006).

3. Emphasis

Generally, the beginnings and ends of sentences, paragraphs, and documents are places of emphasis.[21] They are the places where readers are paying the most attention. Use those places to your advantage. We have mentioned on several occasions in this book that letters and e-mail messages ought to begin with a summary or with a statement of the key information. The same technique can work within the parts or sections of a motion. Place important information at the beginnings and ends of sections and paragraphs. For example, to emphasize a fact, begin with it and reprise it at the end; to de-emphasize a fact, mention it once in the middle of a paragraph.[22]

You can create emphasis with detail. Using specific details tends to draw more attention than using generalities. "It was 17 degrees" is more emphatic than "it was very cold." Of course, excessive details can backfire, becoming tedious and annoying. Besides using detail, you can emphasize a person or entity by making it the subject of several sentences. The person or thing in the subject position of a sentence will appear to be responsible — after all, it is doing the action of the sentence.

Contrary to what you might think, using modifiers and intensifiers like "very," "extremely," and "highly" generally does not create emphasis or persuade a sophisticated reader like a judge. Nor does the use of "loaded" words like "clearly," "obviously," and "blatantly."[23]

D. Anticipate the Response

As the movant, you have an advantage: you get to go first. The judge will, in all likelihood, read the motion before reading the response. That means you get to present the facts and the law favorably to your side before your opponent gets the judge's attention.

Don't waste that advantage by presenting only your client's side. Instead, anticipate your opponent's response and address it in your motion as well. That way, by the time the judge reads the response, the judge will already know what you have to say about it — and, you hope, will be predisposed to your side.

This doesn't mean, though, that you need to spell out your opponent's argument in your motion. Too many motions waste precious moments of their reader's attention, arguing for the other side. In other words, don't do this:

> Chef Luna may argue that because Jackson had used her Twitter account to advertise drink specials and bands in the past, Casa Rita had implicitly authorized her actions. However . . . .

---

21. David Lambuth, *The Golden Book on Writing* 9, 26 (2d ed., Penguin Books, Ltd. 1983).

22. Mary Barnard Ray & Barbara J. Cox, *Beyond the Basics: A Text for Advanced Legal Writing* 184–85 (2d ed., West 2003).

23. *See* Mark Painter, *The Legal Writer* 102–04 (2d ed., Jarndyce & Jarndyce 2003).

Instead, do this:

Jackson's occasional mention of her job, including the restaurant's drink specials and bands, to the friends and family members who subscribed to her personal Twitter account did not convert the account into one authorized by Casa Rita.

If you anticipate and respond to your opponent's arguments in your motion, your reader may be thinking, "Yes, but . . ." while reading the response. Don't squander your chance to plant those seeds of doubt in the motion.

VI. Conclusion

Audience and purpose are wrapped together for a motion: You want to persuade the judge to grant the relief you seek. To do that, meet the judge's needs. Tell the judge the necessary information, providing evidentiary and legal support. Use persuasive writing techniques to demonstrate that the relief your client seeks should be granted. For a sample administrative motion, see Appendix J. For a sample substantive motion, see Appendix K.

10

RESPONSES

Responses offer little to gain but everything to lose. You won't win your case with a dazzling response, but you might lose it with a flawed one. In *The Curmudgeon's Guide to Practicing Law*, Mark Herrmann says of defending depositions: "Nothing helpful can come from deposition defense, but you can lose your case in a heartbeat. Defending depositions can feel like lying in a foxhole as the artillery shells land around you."[1] The same can be said of responses.

I. AUDIENCE

The audience for a response is the same as the audience for a motion. You are writing to the judge (and possibly a law clerk). You should expect your opposing counsel to scrutinize your response and point out any flaws to the judge. Your client and the opposing party may read the response, but, again, your primary focus is the judge.

II. PURPOSE

The purpose of a response is to persuade the court not to order something. That "something" is whatever the motion sought. It might be minor administrative relief; it might be an order dismissing your case.

It is the "not" aspect of responses that makes them difficult. It is hard to be persuasive when you are on defense. You don't want to sound defensive, but a

---

1. Mark Herrmann, *The Curmudgeon's Guide to Practicing Law* 72 (ABA 2006).

response that fails to respond to the motion's best arguments might not provide the judge with the information needed to deny the relief sought. The best responses will persuade the judge of both the merits of the respondent's position and the lack of merit in the motion.

Writing Tip — Editing

With a response, as with every document you send out or file in court, your credibility is on the line. Naturally, honesty and thoroughness build credibility with the judge, as does scrupulous care in reporting the facts and the law and in citing both. But your sentence-level writing matters, too. A document with misspellings, grammatical mistakes, or even just random typographical errors can hurt your credibility. You've got to become proficient at proofreading and editing. Here are some tips:

Leave Enough Time to Edit

How much time should you spend on editing (revising and polishing)? The pros recommend that half the total writing time should be spent revising and polishing. And that doesn't include proofreading (checking for errors). Debra Hart May, *Proofreading Plain and Simple* 46 (Career Press 1997). Can you afford that? Can your clients? It's up to you. But very few lawyers can produce high-caliber work on the first draft. Every good legal writer knows that mediocre writing becomes good writing only after editing.

Assemble Reliable Sources

Don't guess about word usage, punctuation, grammar, capitalization, and other legal-writing conventions. Look it up. Get a good English dictionary and a good legal dictionary (like *Black's Law Dictionary*, 9th edition). Use a reliable style reference, such as Bryan A. Garner, *The Redbook: A Manual on Legal Style* (2d ed., Thomson West 2006), or Anne Enquist & Laurel Oates, *Just Writing: Grammar, Punctuation, and Style for the Legal Writer* (3d ed., Aspen Publishers 2009).

Use More Than One Technique

Do you edit on the computer screen? That's fine, but it's not enough. Do some editing on a hard copy, too. You read and react differently to onscreen text and printed text. *See* Robert DuBose, *Legal Writing for the Rewired Brain: Persuading Readers in a Paperless World* (Texas Lawyer 2010).

Do you read the text out loud? That's great too. You're using your ears, not just your eyes, to help you edit. Now go further and have a trusted colleague read it and suggest some edits. Opening yourself up to critique is hard, but it's a sure path to improvement.

Do you read the document in reverse, from the last sentence to the first? Good. This technique tricks your mind so you're not familiar with the text. Familiarity leads to poor editing. But now read only the topic sentences. Then re-read the opening and closing paragraphs.

III. COMPONENTS OF A RESPONSE

The local rules that control a motion will also control the response. Follow them. You can expect your response and its related documents to include the following components.

A. Caption

The same caption as in all court documents prepared in the case should be at the top of the response.

B. Title

The title should identify who is filing the response and to what it responds. Long motion titles can be shortened as long as the clerk will be able to identify the match for the response.

C. Opening

Presumably the judge will read the motion before reading the response. So the response does not have the same burden the motion has to identify the subject matter. Instead, the response should immediately tell the judge why the relief the motion seeks should not be granted. Your answer to the question, "Why should this motion be denied?" should be the opening sentence or paragraph of your response.

D. Introduction or Preliminary Statement

The motion should have given the judge the context to understand how the relief the motion seeks fits into the overall case. If the motion failed to give that background, the introduction to the response should. That will allow you to set yourself up as the judge's guide through the complexity of the case.

Even if the motion did put the current issue in the larger context of the case, as the respondent's lawyer, you are unlikely to agree with movant's version. Use your introduction to frame the current issue and the case favorably for your client.

Here's how the respondent might introduce its response to the motion that was introduced in the previous chapter:

Introduction

Eduardo Ramirez's deposition is necessary to determine the scope of actual and implied authority given to managers of restaurants in the Festive Foods chain. In this libel action, Casa Rita seeks to avoid liability for a Twitter message sent by its Madison City manager about a drink special at its restaurant. Casa Rita contends that in advertising a drink special at the restaurant she manages, Kim Jackson acted outside the scope of her authority.

Casa Rita cannot simultaneously disclaim responsibility for its manager's actions and prohibit Chef Luna from deposing the manager's supervisors to determine what responsibilities she was given. Although Mr. Ramirez may not be involved with the day-to-day operations of the Madison City Casa Rita, he does oversee operations of all restaurants in the Festive Foods chain. Chef Luna should be allowed to depose Mr. Ramirez to determine what authority Casa Rita managers have.

E. Statement of Facts

In your statement of facts, explain the facts pertinent to the motion as well as any facts pertinent to additional issues you raise in the response. For example, if the plaintiff sought a summary judgment on the substance of the case and the defendant relied on a limitations defense in response, the response's statement of facts should address both the facts relevant to the plaintiff's case and the facts relevant to the defense.

Restating the facts relevant to the motion is worth the effort, both to put your spin on the facts and to keep the judge from having to refer to the motion for an explanation of the relevant facts. If the response relies on different facts (or a different version of the facts) than the motion, those facts will need to be supported by evidence, with citations to that evidence included in the statement of facts. For example, the facts section of the response to the motion seeking to prevent the taking of a company president's deposition might look like this:

Facts

Kim Jackson sent a message through Twitter stating, "Health department's taking over Chef Luna's kitchen. While he's shut down, margaritas are half price at Casa Rita." (Aff. Henry Andrews (Sept. 20, 2011), attached as Exhibit A.) Kim Jackson is the manager of the Madison City location of Casa Rita restaurant. (Transcr. Depo. Kim Jackson 3:21-4:1 (Aug. 15, 2011), attached as Exhibit B.) As such, Ms. Jackson is the highest authority at the Madison City Casa Rita. (*Id.* at 21:7-15.) Casa Rita has taken the position in this lawsuit that it is not liable because Ms. Jackson's message was outside the course and scope of her employment. (Def.'s Answer (July 19, 2011).)

Ms. Jackson's authority to operate Casa Rita is granted by the "home office" of Casa Rita's parent company. (Exhibit B at 33:14-19.) Festive Foods is the Delaware corporation that owns Casa Rita. (Aff. Eduardo Ramirez (Sept. 13, 2011), attached as Exhibit A to Defendant's Motion for Summary Judgment.) Mr. Ramirez is the president of Festive Foods. (*Id.*) While Mr. Ramirez may not know Ms. Jackson personally, he oversees all the company's operations. (*Id.*)

When asked at her deposition who her ultimate boss was, Ms. Jackson responded "Eduardo Ramirez." (Exhibit B at 71:5-8.) Ms. Jackson also stated, "I guess all my authority really comes from him [Mr. Ramirez]." (*Id.* at 72:23-24.)

The failure to cite evidence adequately can hurt your case. One Seventh Circuit case affirmed a summary judgment against a plaintiff after the plaintiff responded to the defendant's motion for summary judgment by providing a narrative statement of facts and citing only once to an entire deposition. Because the court rules required statements of fact in motions and responses to be supported by citations to the record, the trial court deemed the citation to an entire deposition insufficient and treated the defendant's statement of facts as uncontested. Faced with similar deficiencies in the appeal, the Seventh Circuit affirmed the summary judgment and tacked on a fine for the lawyer.[2] To avoid a similar fate, meet any evidentiary burden for your response with care.

F. Motion Standard

Although the motion should contain the standard that the judge must apply in deciding the motion, the response should use the motion standard section to emphasize aspects of the standard that favor the nonmovant. For example, a response to a motion for summary judgment may note that the procedure requires the court to accept evidence favorable to the nonmovant as true and make reasonable inferences in favor of the nonmovant.

G. Argument and Authorities

Use the argument and authorities section to prove why the court should deny the relief the motion seeks.

For administrative matters, a response's argument is typically fact-laden. The court probably has the discretion to grant the relief sought. (If it doesn't, of course, the response should cite legal authorities to prove that.) The court will decide whether use of that discretion would be fair and just. The response needs to show that it would not be fair and just. For example, if the motion seeks a continuance, the response may show why a delay would be unfair to the respondent. If the motion seeks to compel discovery of documents, the response may highlight the unjust burden the discovery would impose on the respondent. Because administrative matters are rarely the subject of appeals, case law addressing the matter is likely to be scarce, leaving you to argue about the facts.

The argument in a response to a substantive motion will focus on both facts and law. Typically, the response will need to show how something — often a pleading, evidence, or an expert's testimony — meets a legal standard.

If you are responding to a motion to dismiss for failure to state a claim, you will need to demonstrate the adequacy of your pleading. While the United States Supreme Court has recently tightened its interpretation of federal pleading

---

2. *Day v. N. Ind. Pub. Serv. Corp.*, 164 F.3d 382, 383–85 (7th Cir. 1999).

standards,[3] the rules themselves remain unchanged. Federal Rule of Civil Procedure 8 requires the complaint to contain "a short and plain statement of the claim showing that the pleader is entitled to relief." A response to a motion to dismiss for failure to state a claim should explain this standard — preferably using cases where the dismissal of a complaint has been reversed. Then, the response should demonstrate why the complaint meets the standard.

If you are responding to a motion for summary judgment, you will need to demonstrate either (1) that your evidence creates a fact issue or (2) that the movant's evidence fails to prove that the movant is entitled to judgment as a matter of law. (Early in the case you may also ask that the motion be denied or a continuance be granted under Federal Rule of Civil Procedure 56(f) or an equivalent rule in your jurisdiction to allow time to obtain the evidence needed to oppose the motion.)

In meeting your burden in responding to a summary judgment motion, your response might try to prove facts contrary to those asserted in the motion, emphasizing the motion standard that factual disputes must be resolved in favor of the nonmovant. Indeed, responses thick with attached evidence are often submitted under the theory that "there must be a fact issue in there somewhere." The response could also attack the adequacy of the evidence attached to the motion or the credibility of the movant's evidence — and remind the court that the fact finder assesses credibility. Or the response might object to the evidence offered with the motion — because it is hearsay, for example. In that instance, determine whether you need to file a motion to strike the offending evidence, in addition to pointing out the inadequacy of the evidence in your response.

If you are responding to a motion to exclude an expert witness, your response needs to prove the admissibility of the expert's testimony. In federal court, the response should explain the standards set forth in *Daubert v. Merrell Dow Pharmaceuticals*[4] and demonstrate how the expert's testimony satisfies those standards. The common refrain of a response promoting the admissibility of an expert's testimony is that any alleged deficiencies in the testimony go to the weight the fact finder should give the testimony, not to its admissibility.

Like a motion, a response should be organized around the issues the court will need to decide. Even if the motion has already provided the court with an overview of the law, the response should provide its own overview, stated as favorably as possible to the respondent's position. That overview should identify elements or issues not disputed in the motion, which will therefore not be discussed in the response. The response should then provide a roadmap, indicating the order in which the response will address the contested issues.

---

3. *See Bell Atlantic Corp. v. Twombly*, 550 U.S. 544, 563 (2007).
4. *Daubert v. Merrell Dow Pharmaceuticals, Inc.*, 509 U.S. 579 (1993).

The previous chapter contained a roadmap for a motion; here's a sample roadmap for a response to that motion:

> Fact issues prevent a summary judgment against Katie Kelley's claim for public disclosure of embarrassing private facts. This tort has three elements: (1) publicity was given to matters concerning one's personal life, (2) publication would be highly offensive to a reasonable person of ordinary sensibilities, and (3) the matter publicized is not of legitimate public concern. *Star-Telegram, Inc. v. Doe*, 915 S.W.2d 471, 473–74 (Tex. 1995). Rick Stafford does not deny in the motion that he gave publicity to matters concerning Ms. Kelley's personal life. The summary judgment evidence raises fact issues about whether publication of the facts regarding the attack on Ms. Kelley would be offensive to a reasonable person and whether the matter was of legitimate public concern. Because of these fact issues, the court should deny the summary judgment motion.

Also, like a motion's argument, a response's argument about each contested issue should follow the classic organizational structure for a legal analysis. After asserting your conclusion on the issue, you should state and explain the governing law. While the motion will also have explained the law, the response should highlight aspects of the law favorable to the respondent. Where possible, appellate cases reversing trial courts for granting similar motions should be used to explain the law. The subtle subtext of the response will be that the court risks reversal if it grants the motion.[5] The law should then be applied to your facts, with fact-based comparisons demonstrating why the motion should not be granted. Wrap up your discussion of each issue by restating your conclusion and tying it back to the reason the motion should be denied.

Writing Tip — Avoiding the Appearance of Sexism

Today, careful writers avoid sexism and even the appearance of sexism. Careful litigators do, too. You should never refer to a "lady lawyer" or a "woman doctor," of course. And you might prefer "chair" to "chairman," "spokesperson" to "spokesman," and "firefighter" to "fireman."

But there's another aspect to nonsexist writing: the male pronoun. Many writers prefer to avoid defaulting to the male pronouns *he*, *him*, and *his* in litigation documents. If you prefer to avoid the default male pronoun, here are some suggestions.

- Don't refer to a singular noun with a plural pronoun. This is still incorrect in professional writing: *A judge can always change their mind.*
- Use paired male-female pronouns sparingly. Using "he or she" occasionally might be fine, but repeated use is distracting. We also recommend against

---

5. Herrmann, *supra* note 1, at 4.

using "he/she" and "s/he." Although they might be conventional in other genres of writing, they are still less than desirable in legal writing.

- Try writing around the male pronoun when you can. Repeat the noun, make it plural, or rephrase the sentence. That way you avoid the problem without drawing attention to the fact that you're avoiding the problem. That's why we don't recommend simply switching to the default female pronoun — it draws attention to the fact that you're avoiding the male pronoun.

What's more, you might avoid the problem this way: Remember that in most litigation writing, you'll have a specific person in mind, even if you're stating a generic legal rule. For example, if you're stating a rule for testamentary capacity, you're envisioning that rule as applied to the particular testator in your case.

If the testator is a woman named Nancy Wright, you might naturally phrase the legal rule this way: "To prove that the testator had testamentary capacity, the proponents must show that she was of sound mind. [citation]." Using the female pronoun here is appropriate because the actual testator in your case is a woman. The reader already has *her* in mind.

Also, we think *testator* covers both men and women, and that *testatrix* and other *-trix* words are unnecessary.

H. Prayer (Also Called "Relief Sought")

The response should ask the court to deny the relief the motion seeks. For example, your prayer on a response might say, "Plaintiff Jackson asks the court to deny Defendant ABC Company's motion for summary judgment."

I. Signature Line

This should match the signature line in your complaint or answer.

J. Certificate of Service

If you copy a certificate of service from a prior document in the case, update it to specify the response being served, how it is being served, and upon whom it is being served.

K. Evidence

If the response challenges only whether the movant is entitled to the relief sought based on the evidence attached to the motion, the response may not need to include any evidence. In other words, if the response argues that even if all the evidence attached to the motion is assumed to be true, the motion should not be granted, then the response will not have to be supported by evidence.

Frequently, however, the response will contest the truth of evidence attached to the motion or will rely on other facts to defeat the motion. In those situations, every fact relied upon in the response must be proved by evidence.

IV. STRATEGIC CONSIDERATIONS FOR RESPONSES

The inherently defensive posture of responses makes them difficult to write persuasively. The movant gets to give the court its initial impression of the controversy. The respondent may seem to be hollering "not" in response. Careful consideration of the order of your arguments and emphasis on the motion standard can help counteract the movant's apparent advantage.

A. Order Your Arguments to Persuade and Respond

The best order for arguments in a response is controversial. From a judge's perspective, a response that tracks the order of arguments in the motion is the most helpful.[6] The judge can easily find the respondent's argument that corresponds to each of the movant's arguments. Since your primary audience member is the judge, ordering the arguments in the manner most helpful to that audience member may seem like the obvious choice. Why, then, is there a controversy?

The controversy arises because although the judge is your primary audience member, your purpose is not to help the judge but to persuade the judge. To persuade the judge, the conventional wisdom is that you should start with your strongest argument.[7] Presumably the movant has ordered its arguments so that its strongest argument appears first. If you respond in the same order, the movant's strongest argument — your weakest — will be first. There, in a position of prominence, where you have the reader's attention, you risk sounding defensive.

As with many other questions in the law, the answer to the question of how to resolve this controversy is "it depends." If your arguments and the movant's arguments are relatively equal in strength, tracking the movant's order of arguments may be worth the points you will score for organizing in a way that is helpful to the judge. If following the movant's order will detract from your strongest arguments, you may reorder the arguments so that your best points come first. In some instances, your opponent may have argued something that seems

---

6. Irwin Alterman, *Plain and Accurate Style in Court Papers* 103 (ALI-ABA 1987) (noting that judges appreciate points following the same order as the main document).

7. *See* Mary Barnard Ray & Barbara J. Cox, *Beyond the Basics: A Text for Advanced Legal Writing* 228 (2d ed., Thomson West 2003) (recommending that an argument section start "with your strongest argument unless logic requires you to modify this approach"); Laurel Currie Oates, Anne Enquist & Connie Krontz, *Just Briefs* 43 (Aspen Publishers 2008) (stating that a trial-brief writer will "almost always set out your own arguments first").

compelling, making it difficult for the judge to concentrate on your argument until that point is addressed. In such an instance, follow the recommendation of Supreme Court Justice Antonin Scalia and writing expert Bryan Garner: "[Q]uickly demolish that position to make space for your own argument."[8]

Whichever order you select, use headings, roadmaps, and thesis sentences that make it easy for the judge to locate your response to each point in the motion. That way, even if you have decided to favor persuasion by putting your strongest argument first, the judge will still turn to your response as a helpful guide because each responding point can be found easily.

Even if one of the movant's arguments seems off point, inconsequential, or unconvincing, briefly explain why. The judge needs to know how to address such points while ruling in your favor.

Writing Tip — Use of Footnotes

Generally, motions and responses should not place text in footnotes. Placing lots of text in footnotes will make the motion or response look like a law review article, a form that is not likely to impress judges. Some judges even denounce textual footnotes. See quotations collected in Bryan A. Garner, *The Winning Brief: 100 Tips for Persuasive Briefing in Trial and Appellate Courts* 140–41 (2d ed., Oxford U. Press 2004).

But we believe there is at least one legitimate reason for putting text in a footnote: You want to respond to a minor point your opponent raised, but you don't want to let that point derail your current argument.

Even with this use of footnotes, though, be brief, and be sure your argument makes sense even if the reader skips the text in the footnote.

B. Emphasize the Motion Standard

While the movant has the advantage of writing first, the response to a substantive motion usually has its own advantage: the procedural posture. The author of a motion to dismiss is asking the court to toss the case based only on the pleadings; the respondent just wants a chance to prove its case. The author of a motion for summary judgment is asking the court to rule against the case as a matter of law; the respondent just wants to present evidence to the fact finder. The author of a motion to exclude expert testimony is asking the court to exclude a witness from testifying; the respondent just wants the witness to speak so that the fact finder can evaluate the testimony. And of course, the

---

8. Antonin Scalia & Bryan A. Garner, *Making Your Case: The Art of Persuading Judges* 17 (Thomson West 2008).

author of a dispositive motion is asking the court to risk reversal; the respondent cautions against taking such a risk.

To exploit this procedural advantage, your response should emphasize the procedural posture. When responding to a motion to dismiss, don't argue the validity of your claim. Simply argue the sufficiency of your pleading.

When responding to a motion for summary judgment, don't argue that your client is right as a matter of law. Simply argue that there is a question of material fact that needs to be resolved by the fact finder. For example, in response to a motion for summary judgment asserting that there is no causation as a matter of law, you do not need to assert that there is causation. You only need to show how the evidence creates a fact issue about whether causation exists.

When responding to a motion to exclude expert testimony, don't argue that your expert is right or that the expert's testimony means your client wins. Instead, show how your expert's testimony meets the standards for admissibility, leaving for another day the argument about the credibility and weight to be given the testimony.

If you argue more than you need to in a response, the judge may find your position unpersuasive. If you modestly assert that the case needs to be allowed to proceed, while subtly reminding the judge of the risk of reversal if this is the end, the judge may see things your way.

V. Conclusion

You won't win your case with a stellar response. But if you marshal your evidence and organize your arguments to show the other side of the movant's story, you may be able to dodge the artillery shells and fight on for another day. For a sample response, see Appendix L.

11

SUPPORTING EVIDENCE

You will need to support most motions and responses with evidence. You will have created or discovered much of that evidence during the course of the litigation. You will create other evidence — usually in the form of an affidavit — specifically for the motion or response.

I. AUDIENCE

Just as with motions and responses, the main audience for supporting evidence is the judge and possibly the judge's law clerk. Your opposing counsel will also read the evidence, hoping to find that it offers inadequate support for the motion or response. The parties may read the evidence as well.

For affidavits, there's another key "audience" member — the person who will sign the affidavit, called the "affiant." That person will be the ostensible author of the document, not really an audience member. But because lawyers frequently draft affidavits for the potential affiants — with the hope that they will agree to sign the affidavit — you must write the affidavit with that crucial person in mind.

II. PURPOSE

The purpose of the evidence is to prove the factual basis for the motion or response. You'll need to attach evidence only to motions that require proof. For example, a motion to dismiss for failure to state a claim will rely on the inadequacy of the complaint, not on separate evidentiary support. Some administrative motions, such as a motion to exceed a page limit, may also not require evidence. But for substantive motions that rely on facts, you'll need evidence to support each factual assertion. Likewise, responses that rely on a different version of the facts to justify denial of the motion need evidentiary support for each factual assertion.

After you've gathered all the evidence supporting the motion or response, reconcile the evidence with the statement of facts in the motion or response. Prove each sentence in the statement of facts with the evidence and, ideally, cite that evidence after each sentence.

III. TYPES OF EVIDENCE

Although other types of evidence may also be included, you'll support a motion or response primarily with the evidence you gathered during discovery.

A. Live Testimony

Some motions will require a hearing at which live testimony will be introduced. For example, a hearing on a motion to modify a child-custody order or a hearing on a request for a preliminary injunction may resemble a trial. For such motions you will not attach the evidence to your motion, although you must still think through how you'll prove each factual allegation in your motion.

B. Deposition Testimony

Portions of deposition transcripts are frequently attached to motions and responses. Indeed, key concessions in a deposition may form the foundation of a summary judgment motion or a motion to exclude expert testimony.

When attaching deposition testimony to a motion, be sure to include all the necessary parts of the transcript. Include the title page and the place where the oath is administered to the witness. Include the portion of the deposition explaining the witness's connection to the case. For example, is the witness the president of the defendant corporation? Did the witness see the accident in question? Failure to include that testimony could result in faulty proof for the motion. For example, a concession that the plaintiff company didn't suffer any damages from the defendant's breach of contract is rendered meaningless if you fail to include proof of the deponent's role as chief financial officer for the plaintiff.

Obviously, you should also include the testimony directly supporting the factual assertions in the motion or response. But in doing so, try to avoid appearing as if you have plucked the testimony out of context. Provide the surrounding testimony — perhaps including a page or two before and after the key language — so the reader can see the topic being discussed when the statements were made. Finally, include the court reporter's certificate and the witness's signature page.

You might be wondering, "Why not just include the entire deposition transcript?" Depositions are frequently long, touching on many topics. Including an entire transcript not only clutters the court's files — paper or electronic — but also clutters the evidence under consideration with the motion. You may unwittingly create factual disputes or provide evidence for arguments you aren't advancing. Including entire deposition transcripts also adds complexity to the record on appeal, making it possible for an appellate court to reverse the case based on aspects of the record no one was arguing about in the court below. So while your deposition excerpts should be generous enough to support and show context for your factual assertions, they shouldn't add unnecessary facts to the record.

C. Deposition on Written Questions

As discussed in Chapter 6, depositions can also be taken on written questions. You can use the deposition on written questions just like the transcript from a live deposition to provide evidentiary support for a motion or response.

D. Documents

Documents are often attached to motions and responses. Keep in mind, though, that the document alone is likely to prove very little. For example, assume a medical record with the plaintiff's name on it is attached to a summary judgment response. What does the record prove? Without other evidence, it isn't authenticated, so we don't know that it is actually the plaintiff's medical record. It hasn't been proved to constitute a business record, so everything in it is hearsay. Standing alone, the document proves nothing.

You must take care, then, to prove up every document attached to the motion. Most documents will need to be accompanied by an affidavit that authenticates the document. If the document is offered to prove the truth of a matter asserted in it, an affidavit or other testimony may be needed to prove the applicability of a hearsay exception. Only when the document is accompanied by other appropriate evidence will you be able to rely on its contents for proof of facts contained in it.

That being said, you may have some leeway if you are filing an administrative motion. In some courts, it is common practice for lawyers to attach letters between counsel without attaching additional evidence proving up the letters. No one may protest, for example, if a letter to a lawyer is attached as an exhibit to a motion to compel discovery. Check local rules and customs to confirm that such a practice is acceptable.

E. Discovery Responses

If the opposing party has made an admission or stated a fact in response to an interrogatory that supports your motion or response, you can attach the opponent's discovery responses as evidence. You can also attach documents produced in discovery, and under some rules they may be self-authenticating. The key here is that only your opponent's responses, not your own client's responses, should be attached as evidence.

F. Pleadings

Likewise, if your opponent has stated or admitted something in a pleading that supports your motion, you can use that admission as evidence. And again, your own pleadings cannot be offered as proof of the facts you've alleged. You will need an affidavit from your client to prove those assertions.

If the admission appears in an answer that identifies only the paragraph number of the part of the complaint that is admitted, you'll need to cite both the complaint and the answer to prove the admission. The complaint and answer will, of course, be part of the court's file, and an order granting or denying the motion will likely recite that the court considered the pleadings on file in the case. Still, you should determine whether local practice calls for you to attach to your motion or response the pleadings on which you rely. Some courts may consider additional copies unnecessary clutter; others may not want to have to dig through the court's file to find the operative pleadings.

G. Affidavits

If discovery in the case or admissions from your opponent have not provided the evidence you need in support of a motion or response, you'll probably use one or more affidavits to support the statement of facts. An affidavit is a written, sworn statement by a witness, reciting facts that the witness knows. While your client or employees or representatives of your client are the most likely people to sign an affidavit for you, you may also obtain affidavits from third parties. You may not seek an affidavit from a witness whom you know to be represented by counsel unless you go through the witness's lawyer.

All of the other types of evidence in support of motions and responses will have been created at other stages of the case, either as the underlying facts occurred or as the litigation progressed. Affidavits, however, you may draft at the motion stage. We will turn, then, to the components of affidavits and to strategic considerations for drafting them.

IV. COMPONENTS OF AN AFFIDAVIT

Some components of an affidavit are required by law; others are simply included by tradition. While it is likely safe to omit some of the traditional verbiage, lawyers are loath to risk reversal by leaving off language that is harmless to include.

Writing Tip — Avoiding Legalese

Preparing an affidavit presents the litigation writer with ample opportunities to use legalistic terminology, archaic verbiage, and insider legal jargon. But remember: The affiant will quite often be a nonlawyer who is unfamiliar with legal language. And more to the point, the affiant is the one actually "speaking" through the affidavit, even if a lawyer wrote it. "An affidavit, of course, is supposed to be the words of the person offering it." Steven D. Stark, *Writing to Win: The Legal Writer* 167 (Doubleday 1999).

No matter how you prepare an affidavit, avoid the excesses of legalese. For example, we've been asked to referee debates about whether the affidavit should conclude with

FURTHER AFFIANT SAITH NAUGHT

or

FURTHER AFFIANT SAYETH NOT

What's the right answer? Delete this meaningless phrase from your affidavits and use "signed." *See* Joseph Kimble, *Nuts to "Further Affiant Sayeth Naught,"* Mich. B. J. 48 (Sept. 2004).

Other words and phrases to omit from affidavits:

For		prefer	
For	*duly sworn*	prefer	*sworn* or *under oath*
For	*deposes and says*	prefer	*states*
For	*affirm*	prefer	*state*
For	*herein*	prefer	*here* or *in this affidavit*
For	*the undersigned*	prefer	*me* or *[notary public's name]*
For	*subscribed*	prefer	*signed*

Some advice for the novice litigation writer: You might be working from a form affidavit that contains archaic legalese, and for various reasons you might decide to leave the legalese unchanged. For example, it might not be cost effective to take the time necessary to change the language, or your supervisor may prefer the traditional legalese. In those cases, you might need to stick with the legalese. *See* Wayne Schiess, *When Your Boss Wants It the Old Way*, 12 Scribes J. Leg. Writing, 163, 165–66 (2008–2009); Wayne Schiess, *What to Do When a Student Says "My Boss Won't Let Me Write Like That,"* 11 Persps.: Teaching Leg. Research & Writing 113, 114 (2003).

But you might also take advantage of some recent research showing that a majority of judges prefer a modern, direct writing style without legalese. Sean Flammer, *Persuading Judges: An Empirical Analysis of Writing Style, Persuasion, and the Use of Plain English*, 16 Leg. Writing 183 (2010).

A. Caption

The same caption as in all court documents prepared in the case should be at the top of the affidavit. Sometimes a witness may sign an affidavit not in conjunction with a particular case; if so, no case caption will be included on the document.

B. Title

The title should identify the affiant. The affidavit may be labeled simply "Affidavit of Jennifer Randall." If the affidavit is written in support of a particular motion or response, you can include that information in the title. For example, the affidavit may be called "Affidavit of Jennifer Randall in Support of Matthew Bryson's Response to Carrington Display's Motion for Summary Judgment."

C. State and County Identification

The state and county in which the affidavit is signed are typically identified near the top of the affidavit.

D. Name and Qualifications of Affiant

The opening text of the affidavit should identify the affiant and state the affiant's qualifications to give the affidavit. Typical language states the affiant's name, that the affiant is more than 21 (or 18) years old, that the affiant has not been convicted of a felony, and that the affiant has personal knowledge of the facts stated in the affidavit. Because the rules regarding qualification of witnesses vary, affidavits usually generically state that the affiant is "otherwise qualified to make this affidavit" or suffers "no legal disabilities" and is "competent to testify."

E. Basis for Affiant's Knowledge

Next, the affidavit should identify the affiant's connection to the case — how this person knows what is about to be stated. While the opening will generically assert that the affiant has personal knowledge of the facts stated in the affidavit, to avoid an objection that that assertion is conclusory, the affidavit should actually state the facts that give the affiant personal knowledge. Perhaps the affiant is the custodian of the records the affidavit proves up. Perhaps the affiant was a witness to the accident in question. Or perhaps the affiant is the plaintiff's treating physician. Tell the reader why the affiant knows the facts contained in the affidavit. Even if the basis for the affiant's personal knowledge isn't contained in the statement of facts of the motion or response, you should explain that basis in the affidavit itself.

Here's how a third-party witness might explain his connection to a case:

> I am a resident of Madison City, Jefferson. I frequently dine at restaurants, including Luna Azul and Casa Rita, two Mexican-food restaurants in Madison

City. Last year I learned that the manager of Casa Rita, Kim Jackson, had established a Twitter account called @JacksonRita. She used the account to send messages about drink specials and bands playing at Casa Rita. I thought it would be fun to get those kinds of updates, so I signed up to follow the @JacksonRita account.

F. Facts

The bulk of the affidavit will state the facts the affidavit is being used to prove in support of the motion or response. The affidavit should be written in the first person, told from the affiant's point of view. A routine affidavit, such as one used to prove up business records, may contain fairly formulaic language proving the necessary facts. The affidavit of a key witness will contain more detail about the facts at issue.

Here's how the same third-party witness might continue his testimony:

> On February 11, 2010, I read one of the @JacksonRita messages. It said "Health department's taking over Chef Luna's kitchen. While he's shut down, margaritas are half price at Casa Rita." I knew that Chef Luna owned Luna Azul, so I understood the message to mean that Luna Azul had been closed by the Health Department.
>
> I'm pretty sensitive when it comes to health issues, so I was disturbed by the message. I decided not to go back to Luna Azul. I visited Casa Rita on February 27, 2010, and the half-price margarita special was still going on. At that point I figured that Luna Azul had been shut down for good.

G. Signature Line

The affidavit should contain a signature line for the affiant, with the affiant's name typed under it.

H. Jurat

The jurat is the place where the notary public will sign the document. After confirming the affiant's identity and watching the affiant sign the affidavit, the notary will sign and stamp the affidavit. The jurat looks like this:

Sworn and signed before me, a notary public for the state of [name of state], on [date].

_____
[signature]

[seal]   Printed name: [name]
My commission expires: [date]

Note that in a federal case, if you run into trouble getting an affidavit notarized, you may be able to substitute an unsworn declaration under federal law. Section 1746 of volume 28 of the United States Code provides that when a federal law or rule requires an affidavit, except in certain circumstances, the matter may instead be proved with an unsworn declaration "in substantially the following form":

> "I declare (or certify, verify, or state) under penalty of perjury that the foregoing is true and correct. Executed on (date).
> (Signature)."

V. Strategic Considerations for Affidavits

Affidavits provide an opportunity to have a witness present the facts favorably for your side. You should use them to present your case persuasively, but carefully consider who should draft the affidavit, plan in advance for obtaining affidavits from third parties, and discuss needed testimony with experts before designating them as witnesses.

A. Use Affidavits to Present Your Case Persuasively

An affidavit can be written with your specific motion or response in mind. It can include the facts needed to support the motion or response and omit extraneous information. The story can be presented persuasively, starting and ending with strong points and elaborating on favorable information. Therefore, if you can obtain an affidavit from a witness, that should be your first choice.

For example, your client may have been deposed in the case. Since the attorney conducting the deposition presumably asked your client about the relevant facts, somewhere in the deposition you can probably find the support you need. But why use an excerpt from the deposition transcript? The testimony will be presented in a piecemeal, question-and-answer format, not in the narrative format an affidavit allows. The questions will have been asked by someone who wants to emphasize points contrary to your position and who will usually not let the witness elaborate on the favorable information. The relevant questions and answers will likely be scattered throughout the deposition, rather than presented concisely in a page or two.

An affidavit allows you to remedy all of these flaws, presenting the testimony as you see fit. If the witness is willing to sign an affidavit, have the witness do so rather than rely on deposition testimony.

B. Consider Carefully Who Should Draft the Affidavit

An affidavit drafted by the witness is likely to sound more like the witness (and less like a lawyer). Try as we might to sound like "real people," lawyers too often end up drafting an affidavit that has a different voice than an affidavit drafted by a witness. This might counsel in favor of having the witness draft the affidavit.

But consider the limitations. First, the witness is likely to feel a bit bewildered by the prospect of writing the affidavit. Since it's not an everyday occurrence, the witness won't know where to start or what to include. Second, the witness isn't trained in the law or in persuasive writing. Hearsay or other evidentiary problems may arise, and the facts may not be presented as favorably as possible. Third, asking the witness to write the affidavit imposes a substantial burden on the witness. A witness who is asked to tell the story orally, read an affidavit to confirm that it is accurate, and sign the affidavit may be willing to do so, while the same witness might not be willing to compose the affidavit from scratch. Since the witness is likely to be either your client or a third person over whom you have no control, trying to impose such a burden on the witness isn't a pleasant prospect.

Steven Stark suggests an approach that overcomes these obstacles: recording and transcribing the witness's description of the facts, and then editing it to make it read better.[1] But this approach presents its own strategic limitations. In some jurisdictions, any statement by a witness is discoverable. A recording of the witness's oral statement would have to be produced during discovery. Thus, your opponent will receive both the recording of the oral statement and the final version of the affidavit attached to your motion or response. These can then be picked apart for inconsistencies. If the witness omitted information from the oral statement that you wanted included in the final version, your opponent could use the changes to suggest that the witness added those words only at the behest of counsel and didn't initially recall events that way. If you omitted from the affidavit information that was included in the oral statement, your opponent could suggest that you were trying to withhold information or shape the testimony. In any event, providing your opponent with a recording of the witness's statement is handing the other side fodder for cross examination of the witness.

Finally, what harm comes from having the witness's affidavit written by the lawyer? Stark says that an affidavit written by a lawyer will sound like it is written by a lawyer and thus will be less credible.[2] But if credibility must be assessed, there's a fact issue that will likely cause the motion to be denied anyway. In other words, a judge is not going to say, "This affidavit proves this dispositive fact, and there's no controverting evidence, but the affidavit sounds like it was written by a lawyer so I find it not credible and will deny the motion." The judge will deny the motion if there is controverting evidence, but that will happen whether the affidavit "sounds" credible or not. Since a judge will not be assessing credibility when

---

1. Steven D. Stark, *Writing to Win: The Legal Writer* 167 (Doubleday 1999).
2. *Id.*

deciding whether to grant or deny a motion, any advantage to be obtained from having the witness write the affidavit or give a recorded oral statement is likely outweighed by the limitations of those procedures.

C. Plan in Advance for Obtaining Affidavits from Third Parties

Regardless of who will do the writing, you should plan carefully if you'll need affidavits from third parties or expert witnesses. Usually, obtaining an affidavit from your client or an employee of your client will not be difficult. You'll have interviewed the witness and will be familiar with the facts the witness knows. The witness will have an interest in the litigation and, thus, will be willing to cooperate with you. As long as you leave enough time for the witness to read the affidavit to ensure its accuracy, you should end up with a signed affidavit that supports your motion or response.

A third-party witness, on the other hand, likely does not have an interest in cooperating with you. Most people not involved in litigation would like to stay that way — uninvolved. Therefore, you may need to summon all your advocacy skills to persuade a witness to speak with you, let alone sign an affidavit for you. You may be able to cajole the witness into cooperating by appealing to the witness's instincts to help your wronged (or wrongfully accused) client. You can also remind an uncooperative witness that the alternative to a friendly interview is being subpoenaed for a deposition, which is likely to be a more time-consuming and unpleasant process. (Remember, though, that if you submit an affidavit from a witness, opposing counsel is likely to seek the witness's deposition. Don't promise any tradeoffs you can't guarantee.)

Before you count on obtaining a witness's affidavit, see if the witness is willing to cooperate. Interview the witness before attempting to draft the affidavit. Take careful notes so you can put the affidavit in the witness's words. Then approach the witness with a draft affidavit, but make it clear that the affidavit is only a draft and that you want the witness to be completely comfortable with it before signing. Expect to go through several versions before reaching a draft you and the witness can agree on. (Unlike a draft written by the witness or a recording of a witness statement, a draft of the affidavit that you write and that a witness refuses to adopt will likely be protected from discovery by the work-product privilege.) And don't assume you'll be able to obtain the affidavit until you have it in hand — signed.

D. Discuss the Testimony You Need Before Hiring an Expert

Another pitfall for lawyers trying to get affidavits signed occurs when working with expert witnesses. Lawyers often select expert witnesses when facing a court-imposed deadline for designating expert witnesses. The lawyer will talk to the expert about the case and discuss the expert's opinion. Unfortunately, the conversation may not involve the exact wording of that opinion. Only when it comes time to prepare an affidavit for the expert will the lawyer and the expert discover a gap between what the lawyer wants the expert to say and what the expert is willing to say. For example, in a medical case, the lawyer and the expert may agree that a certain procedure should have been used and that the failure to use the procedure was the cause of the plaintiff's harm. But when it comes time to sign the affidavit, the lawyer may want the expert to put his opinion in terms of a certain standard, such as a "reasonable degree of medical probability." The expert may be unfamiliar with — and uncomfortable using — the legal terminology.

To avoid finding yourself stuck, having designated an expert who can't express an opinion in the terms you believe it needs to be expressed in, have a thorough conversation with the expert before the deadline to designate expert witnesses. Find out exactly what the expert is and isn't willing to say. If the expert isn't willing to adopt your terminology, do some research to determine whether the expert's terminology will satisfy the legal standard you are facing. Don't wait until you need an affidavit to discover the gap in your evidence.

VI. Conclusion

All the evidence attached to a motion will be important to prove to your audience that the facts stated in the motion are true. You will have gathered most of the supporting evidence during the case, but you may need to write affidavits for some witnesses yourself. In doing so, explain the facts relevant to the case — making clear why the witness knows those facts — in language the witness will be comfortable adopting. For a sample affidavit proving up business records, see Appendix M. For a sample affidavit proving facts in the case, see Appendix N.

12

MEDIATION STATEMENTS

The reality today is that few cases go to trial. While some are decided on substantive motions, many are resolved through some means of alternative dispute resolution, such as arbitration or mediation. That means that at some point in the life of your case, you are likely to write a document — perhaps called a "statement," a "report," or a "brief" — explaining your case to a neutral third party. We'll discuss the least formal type of alternative dispute resolution document, a mediation statement, here. You should be able to adapt these basics to whatever form your particular method of dispute resolution requires.

I. AUDIENCE

The primary audience for a mediation statement is, of course, the mediator. Typically the mediator will be selected by the parties, so it may be someone you know. Use that knowledge to tailor your statement to your audience's preferences.

Your client is also likely to read your mediation statement. Because so many cases settle before you get a chance to give your opening statement at trial, your mediation statement may be your best chance to tell your client's story.

Although some mediators ask the parties to exchange written mediation statements, typically your opposing counsel, the opposing party, and the court will *not* be reading your mediation statement. You'll need to check the rules for your jurisdiction, but the confidentiality of mediation statements is often protected by law. That allows you to write candidly, which can help the mediator make an accurate assessment of your case.

II. PURPOSE

The purpose of your mediation statement is to give the mediator the information needed to help resolve the case. The mediator will try to help the parties settle the case by assisting the parties in assessing the value of the case and the likely outcome if the case were to go to trial. That means your mediation statement should provide all the information the mediator needs to make that assessment. In addition to addressing the significant factual and legal contentions the case presents, it should also point out other noteworthy components of the case, such as sympathetic witnesses or damaging evidence.

III. COMPONENTS OF A MEDIATION STATEMENT

The exact form of your mediation statement will vary according to your mediator's preferences. Some mediators will provide a form for counsel to complete; others will list the components they want in your statement. If your mediator does not suggest a format, a letter or memo format should be fine. Whatever form the statement takes, it should include the following components.[1]

A. Introduction

Like many other audience members for legal writing, your mediator is likely to be busy. So at the very beginning of your statement, tell the mediator about the core of the case: Who is claiming what against whom? And, because mediation is, at the end of the day, about getting the case resolved, what does your client think should be done about it?

The introduction should be brief, just a paragraph or two to orient the mediator to the case. For example, the introduction to a mediation statement might look like this:

> Patty Simms sued Apple Tree Foods for violating the Americans with Disabilities Act. Simms, a long-time Apple Tree employee, was injured in a car accident and lost mobility in her legs. Because Simms could no longer perform her duties as a stocker, she sought a transfer to a position as a stockroom clerk. Although Simms was qualified for the position, Apple Tree Foods hired another candidate and demoted Simms to the position of greeter. Apple Tree Foods' refusal to transfer Simms to a vacant position violated her right to an accommodation of her disability under the ADA. Simms seeks transfer to the stockroom clerk

---

1. For a discussion about preparing a mediation statement, *see* Gwendoline Davies, *Preparing for a Successful Mediation*, in *ADR Strategies in the UK: Leading Lawyers on Preparing Clients, Navigating the Negotiation Process, and Overcoming Obstacles* ch. 13 (Aspatore 2008) (available at 2008 WL 5662133, *6).

position and $15,000 in compensation for the income she lost while working in the lower-paying greeter position.

B. Factual Background

Next, you should tell the mediator about the facts of the case. While you aren't making an argument to a jury, you do want to give the mediator a sense of how the case could play out at trial. So take the time to develop the story. Explain who the main players are, providing enough of their background to demonstrate whether they are likely to be sympathetic and credible witnesses. Describe how the facts occurred, providing just enough detail to allow the mediator to see how a jury might react to the story.

Writing Tip — Organizing Facts Chronologically

By the time you're writing the mediation statement, you may have completed discovery—including depositions. So you ought to know the facts well. But the mediator does not, and you must present the facts in an understandable way. A key to making the facts understandable is chronology.

If you're writing a facts statement, you're probably telling a story. Stephen V. Armstrong & Timothy P. Terrell, *Organizing Facts to Tell Stories*, 9 Persps.: Teaching Leg. Res. & Writing (2001). "[S]tories are best told chronologically. Chronology is, then, the bread and butter of fact writers." *Id.* The story may have come to you in bits and pieces, from depositions and documents, but you must consolidate that information, organize it, and present it in a readable narrative. Tell the story in the order it happened, not the order in which you discovered it.

Yet the advice to use chronology does have exceptions.

* You can deviate slightly from chronological order to begin the statement of facts by setting the stage or framing the context. Doing so helps orient the reader to the situation. Then, proceed chronologically. For example, you might open the facts this way: "Patty Simms sued Apple Tree Foods for violating the Americans with Disabilities Act." That sentence sets the stage generally but is obviously not the first thing that happened. Or this: "Business at Luna Azul, a restaurant operated by Plaintiff Chef Luna, dropped dramatically after an Internet post about alleged health code violations at the restaurant." Then, narrate the story of the case chronologically.
* Even in a mediation statement, you might choose to begin the statement of facts by describing an important fact that is favorable to your client or that puts your case in a positive light. Then proceed chronologically.
* Finally, if the statement of facts is long or complex—or both—you might decide to group facts by topic, and you might use subheadings to separate the topics. For example, in stating the facts of a case about an Internet posting by a manager allegedly acting outside the course and scope of

her employment, you might divide the statement of facts into these three topics: the posting, the manager's authority, and the effect of the posting on the plaintiff's restaurant. Naturally, within each topic, you use chronological order.

Even when using chronological order, avoid overusing specific dates. It's common advice to omit a flurry of irrelevant dates: "Avoid over-chronicling — most dates are clutter." Mark Painter, *The Legal Writer* 334–34 (2d ed., 2003). When the specific date isn't relevant, use relative statements of time like "three months later" or "the next day." Use cuing words to tell the story: "first," "next," "later," and the like. And avoid the all-too-common practice of summarizing testimony witness by witness. That approach will surely not be chronological. William Whitbeck, *View from the Appellate Bench: The 10 Biggest Winners*, Student Law. 16, 16 (Dec. 2007) (Judge Whitbeck sits on the Michigan Court of Appeals).

C. Claims and Defenses

After telling the story behind the case, provide a list of the claims and defenses asserted by each party. For each claim or defense asserted by your client, describe the facts supporting it, but acknowledge any holes in the claim. For each claim or defense asserted by the opposing party, identify any weaknesses in the claim, but concede strengths as well. For example, a defendant might write this about a claim asserted by the plaintiff:

> **Bryson's retaliation claim:** Bryson claims that Carrington Display retaliated against him under the Title VII of the Civil Rights Act of 1964. But Title VII states that it is an unlawful employment practice for an employer to discriminate against an employee because "he has opposed any practice made an unlawful employment practice by this subchapter." Bryson does not allege that he opposed an unlawful employment practice; he only alleges that his sister did so. While a few courts have allowed third-party retaliation claims, the majority of jurisdictions that have considered the issue have rejected them.

D. Contested Legal Issues

You should also provide the mediator with a list of the contested legal issues in the case. Some of these, of course, will have already arisen in your list of the parties' claims and defenses. In the section on contested legal issues, you can provide a more complete legal argument for each issue. This will allow the mediator to evaluate your client's likelihood of prevailing on the issue. If a lengthy argument is required, however, consider attaching a separate legal memorandum addressing the issue.

Other contested legal issues central to the case but not listed among the claims and defenses should also be listed and briefly explained in this section. These might include issues such as what jurisdiction's law will apply, whether certain testimony or evidence will be admitted at trial, or how damages will be calculated. For example, a contested legal issue might be described this way:

> **Inadmissibility of handwritten notation:** To prove that she was discriminated against on the basis of her disability, Simms relies on a handwritten notation that appears to contain the word "wheelchair" on her application for the stockroom clerk position. The Apple Tree Foods employee who reviewed all of the applications testified in his deposition that the handwriting was not his. No one has been able to identify the handwriting or to determine when or why the note was written. Because the author of the note is unknown, the note will not qualify as an admission of a party opponent or a business record and should be excluded as hearsay at trial.

E. Relief Sought

Although you will have identified the relief your client is seeking or offering in the introduction to the mediation statement, this section should go into more detail. Explain how you have calculated any damages sought, referring to available documentation to support those damages. If the defendant contests the plaintiff's calculation of damages, this section should explain where the parties differ in their calculations and why your client's calculation is correct. This section should also identify any nonmonetary relief sought.

IV. STRATEGIC CONSIDERATIONS FOR MEDIATION STATEMENTS

Mediation provides a unique opportunity to get a neutral third party's assessment of your client's case. Write the statement to facilitate that process.

A. Assess Your Case Honestly

The mediator does not have any power over the parties and won't "decide" the case. For the parties to reach a settlement, they must come to an agreement about the value of the case. While some lawyers say that a good settlement is one in which both parties walk away unhappy, a mediator can't compel the parties to settle. That means the case will only settle if there is some overlap in the range of values each party assigns to the case. That overlap is likely to occur only if each party has assessed the case honestly.

You will write the mediation statement to inform the mediator about the case, but you can also use it as a tool to evaluate the case yourself. Engaging in that objective assessment before the mediation will put you — and your client — in the best position to decide whether your opponent's offer is worth accepting.[2]

B. Concede Known Weaknesses

The mediator assessment of the parties' prospects at trial can go a long way in convincing the parties to settle. Even though you'll want the mediator to think highly of your case and will present your strongest position accordingly, you'll also need to concede weaknesses in your case. Conceding weaknesses may seem counterproductive, but it can show the mediator that you are capable of accurately evaluating your own case. If you and your client can't acknowledge weaknesses in your case, you are unlikely to evaluate the case realistically. And when the parties aren't realistic about the case's value, settlement is unlikely.

Conceding known weaknesses can also help in another respect. Sometimes a lawyer and a client have differing views about a case's worth or about the significance or insignificance of evidence and issues in the case. Conceding potential weaknesses can allow the mediator to mediate not only between parties, but also between lawyer and client. Perhaps the mediator will convince the pessimistic lawyer that a potential issue isn't as significant as the lawyer fears. Or perhaps the mediator will convince an indignant client that the client's outrage might be justified but nevertheless has little legal value. If the mediation statement candidly concedes weaknesses, the mediator's expertise can be used to help lawyer and client appraise the case the same way.

C. Let Your Client Be Heard

Sometimes clients just want someone to hear their story. For your client, the case may be less about monetary damages than it is about vindication. Strategically, court documents can be a bad vehicle for airing your client's grievances. You risk alienating the judge or jury if your client seems petty or dramatic. Mediation statements don't have the same risk. While you could alienate the mediator, the downside is small. Meanwhile, your client may be more inclined to settle once the client's had its say, even if that say is to a mediator. Having your day in court might be an increasing rarity, but having your say at mediation can be a reasonable substitute.[3] So serve as your client's mouthpiece in your mediation statement. Ask your client to read the mediation statement so the client will see that the story has been told. A good mediator will acknowledge the validity to your client's position during the mediation. Then the client may be ready to move on.

---

2. For more about a mediator's desire that the lawyer assess the case objectively, *see* Wayne Schiess, *Writing for the Legal Audience* 72–73 (Carolina Academic Press 2003).

3. Davies, *supra* note 1.

D. Respect the Mediator's Time

Naturally, you want to be brief when preparing a motion or other pleading; the judge and court staff are busy, with many cases to oversee. Yet your pleadings and supporting documents must be thorough, never omitting crucial information or authority. The same goals hold for mediation statements. Efficiently delivering the key, relevant information to the mediator enhances your credibility and avoids wasting the mediator's time.

Writing Tip — Brevity

Almost any document can be made brief by removing content — but that's not what we mean here. When we advocate *brevity*, we mean a concept that might be better called "concision." You should make the document as brief as possible while retaining the necessary content. In other words, don't make your document shorter by removing content your reader needs. Instead, condense and tighten that content. Our advice:

Don't Fear Possessives
Using possessives is not informal or inappropriate in a mediation statement. If using a possessive will save you words, use it.

employee of Triton	becomes	*Triton's employee*
negligence of the operator	becomes	*operator's negligence*

Prefer the Verb
When you use the noun form of a word that could have been a verb, you're using a "nominalization," and you're usually using more words than you need.

make a payment	becomes	*pay*
enter into an agreement	becomes	*agree*

Use Simple Prepositions
Some prepositions seem to be on steroids. For brevity, use simpler, shorter forms.

in order to	becomes	*to*
in connection with	becomes	*about* or *for*
with a view toward	becomes	*to* or *for*
for purposes of	becomes	*for*

Omit Throat-Clearers
These are the fluffy phrases we often use to add emphasis or to fill space. Your writing will always be more brief, and usually more emphatic, without them. Here are some common throat-clearing phrases to consider cutting:

It should be noted that . . .
It is important to remember that . . .
We feel compelled to point out that . . .

Minimize Long Connectors

Try to avoid weighty conjunctive adverbs like "additionally," "along the same lines," and "moreover." Gerald Lebovits, *Persuasive Writing for Lawyers — Part II*, 82 N.Y. S.B. Assn. J. 64, 65 (Mar./Apr. 2010).

And remember: "Brevity does not require you to compress every argument into shorthand and cut every sentence to twenty words or less. . . . Brevity requires confidence, perhaps even courage." Stephen V. Armstrong & Timothy P. Terrell, *Thinking Like a Writer* 269 (3d ed., Practising L. Inst. 2009). We encourage you to have the courage to be brief.

E. Be Careful About Disclosing Your Bottom Line

Your mediation statement will include a statement of the relief your client is seeking or offering, but be careful about disclosing your bottom line. Regardless of how emphatically you assert that an offer or demand is your "final offer," the mediator may take any dollar figure in your mediation statement as an opening bid. While you and your client should discuss the bottom line before the mediation, it's best not to disclose that information in your mediation statement.

Keep in mind, too, that Model Rule of Professional Responsibility 4.1 prohibits a lawyer from making a false statement of material fact to a third person in the course of representing a client. While the comment to the rule acknowledges that "certain types of statements ordinarily are not taken as statements of material fact" and that "a party's intentions as to an acceptable settlement of a claim are ordinarily in this category," there's no need to walk close to the line with assertions about what your client is willing to pay or accept in settlement.

F. Consider Remedies Other Than Damages

One benefit of mediation is that the parties, rather than a judge or jury, have control over the outcome. Parties can agree to remedies that a court might be reluctant to order.[4] Consider, then, what relief would best suit your client. For example, would your client like an agreement that the children will attend religious services regardless of which parent they are spending the night with? Would your client like the defendant to disclose bonuses awarded to other employees so the client can confirm fair treatment? The best solution for both sides may be one that a court would be unlikely to grant.

---

4. *Id.*

Use your mediation statement to propose nonmonetary relief that might serve everyone's needs.

V. More Documents if Your Case Settles

If your case settles, more writing awaits you. You will need to prepare the appropriate court papers for your jurisdiction — probably some form of a notice of dismissal or an agreed motion to dismiss. That will look like a typical administrative motion. You will also need to get releases from the appropriate individuals and document the settlement with an agreement.

A settlement agreement is not a litigation document. It's a contract. Therefore, the best advice for writing a settlement agreement is: Don't. Get a transactional lawyer to do it. They are, after all, the experts at documenting agreements between parties. Just as you wouldn't counsel a transactional lawyer to write the litigation documents if a deal went awry and ended up in litigation, you shouldn't write the settlement agreement when your litigation turns into a transaction.

If you don't have the luxury of turning the settlement agreement over to a transactional lawyer, you'll need to carefully think through the terms of the agreement. Among the points you should consider are

- Will the settlement amount be paid in full immediately, or will there be a payout over time?
- If there is a payout over time, should there be security for the debt? Or an agreed judgment that can be entered if the paying party defaults?
- What claims are being released?
- Who needs to sign the agreement for the releases to be enforceable?
- Do you want a confidentiality agreement?
- If you do want a confidentiality agreement, do you want a liquidated damages clause in case it is breached?
- Do you want a forum-selection clause? A choice-of-law provision?

A good starting point for drafting your settlement agreement is the annotated model settlement agreement written by George Parker Young, Todd Baker, and Josh Borsellino for the Texas State Bar Litigation Section.[5] To steer clear of potential problems with your settlement, also take a look at the article *Drafting Settlement Agreements: Pitfalls, Traps to Avoid, and Other Do's and Don'ts* in the same publication.[6]

---

5. George Parker Young, Todd Baker & Josh Borsellino, *An Annotated "Model" Settlement Agreement*, 40 Tex. St. Bar Litig. Sec. Rpt. The Advoc. 38 (Fall 2007).

6. James K. McClendon, Kris R. Kwolek & Jesse B. Butler, *Drafting Settlement Agreements: Pitfalls, Traps to Avoid, and Other Do's and Don'ts*, 40 Tex. St. Bar Litig. Sec. Rpt. The Advoc. 28 (Fall 2007).

VI. CONCLUSION

The mediator will appreciate a mediation statement that candidly and briefly describes the facts and the legal issues in the case. Perhaps more importantly, preparing such a document can also prepare you and your client to settle the case. For a sample mediation statement, see Appendix O.

13

Jury Instructions

Jury instructions are the instructions and questions you will ask the court to give to the jury before deliberations begin in a case. The instructions and questions the judge ultimately submits to the jury are also often referred to as "jury instructions." But for clarity's sake, here we'll refer to the instructions and questions given by the court to the jury as the *jury charge* and the instructions and questions submitted to the judge by the parties as *jury instructions*. Your goal when writing your jury instructions is to have those instructions end up in the jury charge.

I. AUDIENCE

There are three separate — and quite different — audiences for jury instructions. The first audience is the trial judge. That judge will decide which of your jury instructions to put in the jury charge. You want the judge to be satisfied that your instructions accurately reflect the law so the judge will use your instructions, rather than your opponent's, in the jury charge.

The second audience is composed of the jurors. You will learn some information about your jurors during voir dire, but it's hard to generalize much about them in advance. You will likely end up with a fairly diverse group of people with various jobs, a range of ages, and a variety of education levels. Some jurors may have advanced degrees; others may not have graduated from high school. Ideally your jury instructions would be intelligible to each juror. But because of the other two audiences, they might not always be.

The third audience for jury instructions is made up of the judges sitting on the appellate court to which your case may be appealed. Jury instructions are a prime target for appellate review, and here's why. Many possible points of appeal after a jury trial are subject to a standard of review that isn't favorable to the appellant. Challenges to the jury's verdict are likely to be subject to a clearly erroneous standard. Challenges to many of the judge's rulings, such as decisions to admit evidence or sustain objections, are likely to be subject to an abuse-of-discretion standard. In contrast, challenges to the wording of the jury charge will probably be subject to a de novo standard. Thus, you should expect to have the judges on the appellate bench examining your jury instructions as well.

II. PURPOSE

The main purpose of your jury instructions is to obtain a verdict that will support a judgment in your client's favor. You need to submit all the instructions and questions necessary to obtain the required findings.

Because of the likelihood of an appeal focused on the jury charge, you should have a couple of other goals in mind as you prepare your jury instructions. First, you need to make sure your instructions are unassailable on appeal if you obtain a verdict in your client's favor. Second, you need to make sure you have submitted correct questions and instructions and made appropriate objections to your opponent's submissions so you have preserved any complaints about errors in the charge if the jury verdict is not in your client's favor.

III. COMPONENTS OF JURY INSTRUCTIONS

The jury instructions as submitted by the parties look somewhat different from the jury charge the judge will give. The judge's charge will begin with a set of standard instructions, which address things such as considering only the evidence admitted during trial and not trading on answers. Most judges have their own form for these standard instructions, and the parties typically do not submit them. The jury charge will then proceed through all the instructions and questions the judge considers appropriate, typically compiled from the jury instructions submitted by the parties. No citations will be included in the jury charge. The jury charge may contain final admonishing instructions after the questions. It will contain a line for the judge to sign the charge when it is given and a place for the jurors to sign if they agree with the verdict.

In contrast, the jury instructions submitted by the parties will typically be a set of proposed instructions, with each proposed instruction or question on a separate page. Authority will be cited for the proposed instructions. The exact configuration of the instructions will vary by jurisdiction, but proposed jury instructions will typically have the following components.

A. Caption

The same caption as in all court documents prepared in the case should be at the top of the first page of the jury instructions.

B. Title of Entire Set of Instructions

On the first page of the jury instructions, use a title that identifies the entire set of proposed jury instructions. For example, you may be submitting "Plaintiff Matthew Bryson's Proposed Jury Instructions."

C. Identification of the Contents of the Document

Before you begin the individual instructions and questions, you'll include a brief statement asking the court to submit your proposed instructions and questions. For example, it might state:

> Plaintiff Matthew Bryson asks the court to submit the following instructions and questions to the jury after the close of evidence in this case.

The identification of the contents of the document may identify the proposed instructions and questions as an attachment to the document, such as "Exhibit A." In that case, following the identification, include a signature line and certificate of service. Otherwise, the next page will include your first proposed instruction. In that instance the signature line and certificate of service will appear at the end of the document.

D. Caption

Each proposed instruction or question is typically submitted on a separate page. (The idea is that the judge or clerk can take apart the proposed jury instructions and compile the court's charge from the individual instructions and questions submitted by the parties.) So the case caption appears again at the top of each page.

E. Title of Particular Instruction or Question

At the top of each page, include a title that identifies the particular instruction or question on that page. For example, one page may be titled "Defendant Carrington Display's Proposed Jury Question Regarding Attorney's Fees."

F. Text of the Proposed Instruction or Question

Under the title, introduce the proposed instruction or question with language such as, "Plaintiff asks the court to charge the jury as follows." Then, in block quotation format, set out the text of the instruction or question you are proposing, exactly as it should be given to the jury. As we'll discuss below, you will typically start with a pattern or form jury instruction, adapting the language as necessary to fit the facts of your case.

If submission of a question is contingent upon the jury's answer to another question, include an instruction that states the conditions under which the jury should answer the question. For example, a jury usually will be asked to answer a damages question only if the jury has found liability. Therefore, you might have an instruction that states:

> If you answered yes to Question 1, then answer the following question. Otherwise, do not answer the following question.

G. Citation to Authority

After the text of your proposed instruction or question, cite the source of your proposed instruction. Just like any other time you state a proposition of law to the court, you need a citation to authority so the court can verify that your statement of the law is correct. The citation may be to a published pattern jury charge. It may be to a statute. Or it may be to a court opinion in which the court made this statement of law or — ideally — approved of a jury charge with this language.

H. Signature Line for the Judge

At the bottom of each page containing a proposed instruction or question, some lawyers will include a signature line for the judge and a place for the judge to indicate whether the proposed instruction was given, rejected, or modified. As a practical matter, though, formal objections to the charge will usually be made on the record, and the judge often won't sign each proposed instruction or question.

I. Additional Questions and Instructions

The proposed instructions will consist of multiple pages in the same format — caption, title, text of proposed instruction or question, citation to authority, and signature line for the judge. Make sure you have included in your proposed jury instructions every instruction and question necessary to support a verdict in your client's favor.

J. Signature Line

If you treat all the proposed instructions as an exhibit to your document, your signature line will appear after the identification of the contents of the document and before your first proposed instruction. Otherwise the signature line will follow all your proposed instructions and questions.

K. Certificate of Service

The certificate of service will follow your signature line, either before the exhibit containing the proposed instructions and questions or at the end of the document.

IV. STRATEGIC CONSIDERATIONS FOR JURY INSTRUCTIONS

The jury charge is where the law of the land meets the facts of a case. The law determines what goes in the charge. The jurors then decide the answers to the questions in the charge based on the facts of the case.

To use your charge strategically, write your proposed jury instructions early. Keep all your audience members and goals in mind. Write to satisfy all three audiences — to the extent possible — and to fulfill your goals of obtaining a verdict that will support an unassailable judgment or preserving error if you need to appeal. If an appellate specialist is available to help, accept the assistance graciously.

A. Write Your Jury Charge Early and Refer to It Often

As you handle a case in the pre-trial process, it is easy to lose sight of the finish line. When all the discovery is done and all the motions have been ruled upon, you need to convince a judge or jury that the case should come out in your client's favor. If you have a jury trial, the jury charge is the document the jury will use in determining who wins and who loses. The words in that charge will control the jury's decision.

To keep your sights on that final result, draft your proposed jury instructions early in the case. Knowing what the jury will be asked at the end of the trial will help focus your discovery (and your settlement negotiations). As the case proceeds, look at your charge often. Are you gathering all the evidence you need to support findings in your favor on those issues? Also, look at them in reverse. Has discovery produced evidence that isn't relevant under your current version of the jury instructions? If so, do you need to amend your pleadings to state new causes of action or defenses? On the other hand, if discovery has left you with evidentiary gaps, or if you see questions you think the jury will answer against you, consider whether a settlement is in your client's best interests.

B. Follow Form or Pattern Jury Charges to the Extent Possible

Many jurisdictions will have form or pattern jury charges that set forth language to be used to charge the jury for common causes of action and defenses. The pattern charges are typically developed by committees and trusted by trial judges. Thus, to satisfy your first audience — the trial judge — follow the form charges to the extent possible. If a lawyer proposes an instruction that deviates from the form, the judge is likely to want to know why and what the form says.

This is not to say that pattern charges are infallible. They aren't. They are only secondary authority. Appellate courts sometimes conclude that the language in a pattern charge is not a correct statement of the law. If you believe that the pattern charge is incorrect, submit the correct language. But be prepared to convince the judge that deviation from the pattern charge is necessary to reflect the law accurately.

C. Make the Instructions as Intelligible as Possible

Because jurors will attempt to decipher the jury charge, you need to make your instructions as intelligible as possible. But trying to satisfy the jurors may interfere with satisfying your other audiences. For example, an intelligible definition of "producing cause" — one that a nonlawyer juror will understand — will likely deviate from the pattern-jury-charge language the trial judge prefers. And a definition of "producing cause" rewritten into plain English may not satisfy an appellate court as a correct statement of the law. Therefore, while you might have the best chance of communicating to the jury with an instruction that deviates from the standard form, that proposed instruction is unlikely to make it past your first audience member and into the charge. And even if it does, it is at risk of being struck down by your third audience, the appellate court.

Writing Tip — Developments in Pattern Jury Instructions

Those who study jury instructions often opine that jury instructions are hard for nonlawyers to understand: "[E]mpirical evidence shows that jurors do not understand the language used [in many jury instructions], how they're structured, or how they're organized." James D. Wascher, *The Long March Toward Plain English Jury Instructions*, 19 CBA Record 50 (Feb./Mar. 2005). "[F]airer trials with more just (correct) results could be expected from more comprehensible jury instructions." Ronald L. Goldfarb & James C. Raymond, *Clear Understandings: A Guide to Legal Writing* 124 (West 1982).

It doesn't have to be that way. It's possible to write jury instructions in modern, clear English. Joseph Kimble, an expert in plain English writing, asserts that "we know two things for sure after 20 years of research: jurors do not understand old-style instructions, and the instructions can be made much clearer through plain-language principles." Joseph Kimble, *The Route to Clear Jury Instructions*, 6 Scribes J. Leg. Writing 163, 164 (1997).

If you want good guidance for preparing jury instruction that nonlawyers can understand, here are some excellent sources:

- Joseph Kimble, *The Route to Clear Jury Instructions*, 6 Scribes J. Leg. Writing 163 (1997).
- Peter M. Tiersma, *Reforming the Language of Jury Instructions*, 22 Hofstra L. Rev. 37 (1993).
- Federal Judicial Center, *Pattern Criminal Jury Instructions*, Appendix A (West 1988 ed.).

But revising pattern jury instructions into plain English in a particular case you are trying is risky. You're working alone, without a committee to review your

---

work. You're working without an expert in plain English — a key person in any plain English revision process. Most important, you're changing the pattern instructions with which the trial judge and opposing counsel are familiar, instructions that (often) have been approved by a state bar committee, instructions that have been used and upheld on appeal. You are risking reversal of any victory you secure for your client.

Your individual efforts to fix the language of pattern jury charges are therefore likely to meet with great resistance and might even harm your case. So we recommend promoting change by working with the bar and the judiciary on pattern charges, rather than deviating from the approved pattern charges in individual cases.

In fact, top-down jury instruction reform has happened and is happening in several states. *See, e.g.,* J. Scott Vowell, *Alabama Pattern Jury Instructions: Instructing Juries In Plain Language,* 29 Am. J. Trial Advoc. 137 (2005); Peter Tiersma, *Communicating with Juries,* 10 Scribes J. Legal Writing 1 (2005–2006) (discussing the California jury instructions project); Wayne Schiess, *The Texas Pattern Jury Charges Plain-Language Project: The Writing Consultant's View,* 60 Clarity 23 (2008).

But you can take some small steps to try to improve the intelligibility of your charge. Place definitions near the instructions to which they pertain, rather than in a list at the beginning of the document that jurors are unlikely to recall when answering a specific question. If an instruction or definition has several alternatives, make the relationships between the alternatives clear. For example, if a deceptive trade practice can be shown in one of three ways, and there are two alternative methods of proving one of those ways, use outlining, numbering, or other graphics to delineate the relationships between the items. Although you probably should not deviate from the standard language, you can use other methods to provide as much clarity as possible.

D. Stick with Language That Has Been Court-Approved

To please your third audience, the appellate court, you'll have to stick to court-approved language for most items in the charge. For example, in Texas for years the term *producing cause* was defined as

> an efficient, exciting, or contributing cause that, in a natural sequence, produces the injury. There may be more than one producing cause.[1]

You'd be hard pressed to find one in ten lawyers who could explain that definition to you, let alone one in a hundred jurors who could understand it. Still, until the Texas Supreme Court recognized that the archaic definition "provide[d] little

---

1. Tex. Pattern Jury Charges — Bus., Consumer, Ins. & Empl. 102.1 (St. B. of Tex. 2002).

concrete guidance to the jury"[2] and updated the definition itself, Texas lawyers stuck with it to avoid reversal on appeal. You can take some comfort in the possibility that your trial judge might let you interpret the term for the jury during your closing argument.

E. Include All Instructions and Definitions Needed to Support a Judgment in Your Favor

The party bearing the burden of proof on an issue usually carries the burden of getting the proper questions submitted to the jury. So if your claim for treble damages requires a finding that the defendant acted willfully, you'll need to submit a proper question asking about willfulness. If your statute of limitations defense requires a finding of the date on which the plaintiff discovered the injury, submit the correct question. If you don't, you will have waived that claim or defense on your client's behalf. Then it's time to call your malpractice insurance carrier.

F. Draft Instructions Even for Questions You Don't Want Submitted

Since you are usually required to draft only the instructions and questions you want submitted, you may be tempted not to draft the instructions and questions pertaining to the other side's claims or defenses. After all, that's their burden, so why do the work for them, right? Wrong.

Even if you are not relying on a question or instruction, if the language isn't correct, you'll need to point out the defect — specifically. If you haven't drafted the questions and instructions in advance, you are less likely to spot such deficiencies. If you object only to submitting the question at all, typically on the ground that there's no evidence to support a finding against you, you will not have preserved any objection to the form of the question. Sure, you will have preserved your "no evidence" objection, but that will leave you with a much harder path on appeal than an objection to the form of a question. That's because, in conducting a "no evidence" review, the appellate court will comb through the record, looking for any evidence that supports the finding against you. In contrast, if you had also objected to the form of the opponent's question and offered an alternative, the appellate court would review the wording of the instruction under a de novo standard. But if you fail to draft the question yourself, and thus fail to notice that the language is objectionable, your objection to the form of the question will be waived.

Let's say, for example, that you represent a defendant in a negligence suit. The plaintiff is seeking punitive damages against your client on the ground that its conduct amounted to gross negligence. It is your position that there is no

---

2. *Ford Motor Co. v. Ledesma*, 242 S.W.3d 32, 46 (Tex. 2007).

evidence of gross negligence and that the question should not be submitted to the jury at all. So you object to the submission of the gross negligence question. But the trial court overrules that objection and decides to submit the question as drafted by the plaintiff. Because you didn't draft your own gross negligence definition, you don't notice the flaw in the plaintiff's definition of gross negligence and don't object to the form of the question. The jury finds gross negligence and awards punitive damages against your client. On appeal, you're left arguing that there's no evidence to support the jury's finding. Your brief will have to discuss all the evidence of your client's less-than-stellar conduct and argue that it doesn't amount to evidence of gross negligence. The appellate court will be deferential to the jury's finding — applying a "clearly erroneous" standard, or a similarly deferential standard of review. Instead, if only you had written your own gross negligence definition and then properly objected to the plaintiff's flawed definition, you could be making a legal argument about the wording of the definition and enjoying the de novo review standard.

Drafting all the instructions and questions for any claim or defense relied upon by any party is worth the trouble.

G. Condition Instructions You Don't Want Submitted on Your Objection

So what should you do with the instructions and questions you have drafted but don't really want submitted? The exact procedure will depend on your local practice. You may be able to keep them in your back pocket and offer them only if the court decides to submit the question or instruction over your objection. You may need to provide them to the court earlier in the process.

Whatever the local practice is, be sure to condition your submission of the correctly worded instruction or question on your objection that the instruction or question should not be submitted at all. For example, you might use language like this:

> Defendant Carrington Display objects to the submission of a question to the jury about gross negligence because there is no evidence of grossly negligent conduct by Carrington Display. If the court overrules this objection, Carrington Display further objects that Plaintiff Matthew Bryson's proposed definition of gross negligence is worded incorrectly. If the jury is to be charged regarding gross negligence over Carrington Display's objection, the definition of gross negligence should be worded as follows.

While you want to preserve your objection to the form of the definition, take care to preserve your objection to the submission of the question at the same time.

H. Enlist the Assistance of an Appellate Specialist

Because the wording of the jury charge is a prime target for an appeal, this is a good place to accept (and even seek out) the help of an appellate specialist.

If you have the opportunity to involve an appellate specialist, let that person draft the charge, or at least refine one you drafted at the beginning of the case.

The charge conference — the discussions with the trial judge about what will go in the jury charge — may come near the end of the trial. Typically the charge will first be negotiated off the record, with the judge trying to construct a charge that is satisfactory to both sides. Then formal objections will be made on the record. Because of the timing of the charge conference, you are likely to have a few other things on your mind, like witness examinations and closing argument. So if you can get an appellate specialist involved, let that person handle the charge conference. That way you can rest assured that the charge is properly worded or that any error is properly preserved.

V. CONCLUSION

The differences between the audience members for jury instructions — the trial judge, the jurors, and the appellate judges — make it hard to write something tailored to all three. Meanwhile, the content of the jury charge is crucial because it will be the document that determines whether the court enters a judgment in your client's favor. Still, while writing the instructions and questions necessary to support your client's causes of action or defenses and objecting to improper wording in your opponent's instructions, keep those audience members in mind. Use approved wording to satisfy the judges and use graphics and directions as possible to help the jurors. For a sample jury instruction, see Appendix P.

Appendices

SAMPLE DOCUMENTS

These samples are provided so that you can see what each of the documents discussed in this text might look like with all of its components put together. Note, though, that these are just samples, not templates or forms. Because of the variety in the facts and issues presented in each case, no sample document should be imitated too closely. It is up to you to consider your audience and your purpose for each document you write—and to draft your document accordingly. In addition, litigation documents will always need to comply with the requirements of the court in which the case is pending. Consult the appropriate rules of procedure, local rules, standing orders, and any other directives from the court when preparing your document.

To emphasize that these samples are not in the precise form mandated by any court, the documents are set in a fictional jurisdiction, the state of Jefferson. But, of course, the hierarchy of authority always matters in the real world. For authority purposes, the documents assume that the case is pending in a federal district court located within the Second Circuit.

Appendices

A. SAMPLE ENGAGEMENT LETTER

Bissell&Forrester, LLP

1000 Poplar Avenue, Suite 200
Davenport, Jefferson 55402

Direct dial: (555) 555-1234

erichards@bissellforrester.com

March 2, 2011

Mr. Mike Carrington
Carrington Display, Inc.
1800 Elmwood Avenue
Davenport, Jefferson 55412

Re: Representation of Carrington Display, Inc.
in *Bryson v. Carrington Display, Inc.*;
Civil Action No. 11-CV-743; United States District
Court for the Northern District of Jefferson

Dear Mike:

I enjoyed meeting with you about the prospect of Bissell & Forrester representing Carrington Display in the lawsuit filed by Matthew Bryson. I appreciate your confidence in our firm.

This engagement letter states the terms of our agreement for Bissell & Forrester to represent Carrington Display. Please read the letter carefully and let me know if you have any questions or concerns. If the letter accurately states our agreement, sign where indicated below and return the letter to me.

Because Bissell & Forrester will not begin representing Carrington Display until we have received the signed engagement letter, we need to receive the letter by Friday to begin preparing Carrington Display's answer in this case.

Scope of representation

Bissell & Forrester will represent Carrington Display in the case styled *Bryson v. Carrington Display, Inc.*; Civil Action No. 11-CV-743; United States District Court for the Northern District of Jefferson, and in any appeal arising from this case. This engagement letter covers only the Bryson case. If Carrington Display would like Bissell & Forrester to represent it in any other

---

154

matters, I will be happy to discuss the representation with you. Before we will begin representing you in other matters, Bissell & Forrester and Carrington Display will need to sign a separate engagement letter for each matter.

Bissell & Forrester's obligations

Bissell & Forrester will zealously represent Carrington Display's interests in this case. Of course, outcome in legal matters are never certain and we cannot guarantee a victory.

In addition, Bissell & Forrester will

- inform Carrington Display of all significant developments in this case,
- consult with you on significant decisions about the defense or settlement of this case, and
- protect confidential information provided by Carrington Display as allowed under the attorney-client privilege.

Bissell & Forrester will not represent any party with an interest adverse to Carrington Display in this case.

If Carrington Display decides that it no longer wants Bissell & Forrester's representation in this case, upon notice of that decision Bissell & Forrester will promptly return the case files and cooperate in transferring the representation to the new counsel.

Carrington Display's obligations

Carrington Display will

- provide Bissell & Forrester with complete and accurate information needed in the defense of this case,
- cooperate with Bissell & Forrester in obtaining the information needed in the discovery and defense of this case,
- cooperate with Bissell & Forrester in scheduling matters related to this case, and
- pay—within 30 days—all bills for services rendered in this case.

Termination of representation

Carrington Display can decide at any time that it no longer wants Bissell & Forrester to represent it in this case. If Carrington Display notifies Bissell & Forrester of that decision, Bissell & Forrester will promptly withdraw as counsel in the case. Bissell & Forrester can decide at any time that it will no longer represent Carrington Display in this case. If Bissell & Forrester makes that decision, the firm will promptly notify Carrington Display.

Compensation

Carrington Display will pay Bissell & Forrester for its representation in this case based on the time spent by Bissell & Forrester personnel multiplied by the hourly rate for those personnel. Time will be recorded in increments of 1/10th of an hour. Bills will be sent monthly.

The hourly rates for personnel currently anticipated to work on this case are:

Eva Richards, partner	$350 per hour
Eduardo Martinez, associate	$250 per hour
Sarah Kerr, legal assistant	$150 per hour

Bissell and Forrester will staff the case as efficiently as possible and may use additional or different personnel as needs arise.

The hourly rates of personnel are reviewed annually on February 1 and may be increased. If the rates increase, Bissell and Forrester will notify you 30 days before the rate changes go into effect.

Other costs

Carrington Display will reimburse Bissell & Forrester for payment of other costs associated with this case, including filing fees, travel and parking expenses, court reporter charges, postage, copying charges, delivery charges, certain meals and hotel expenses, and computerized legal research expenses. Bissell & Forrester will detail these expenses on the monthly bills. If it is necessary to engage any expert witnesses in this case, Carrington Display will enter a contract directly with the expert and will be responsible for paying the expert's fees.

Complaints

I hope you will be satisfied with Bissell & Forrester's services in this case. If at any time you have any concerns about how this case is being handled, please let me know. You are also welcome to call Cameron Forrester, the firm's managing partner, with any concerns you have. You can reach him at (555) 555-1111.

Beginning our representation

If this letter accurately states our agreement regarding Bissell & Forrester's representation of Carrington Display in the Bryson case, please sign below and return this letter to me. Because we cannot begin working on the answer to Mr. Bryson's complaint until we receive the signed letter, please return the letter to me by Friday, or let me know if you have decided not to hire Bissell & Forrester.

I look forward to working with you.

Sincerely,

Eva Richards

By: Eva Richards
For the Firm

Agreed:

_____

Carrington Displays, Inc.
By Mike Carrington, President

Date: _____

B. SAMPLE DEMAND LETTER

Martin & Associates P.C.

1250 Monroe Street, Suite 311
Davenport, Jefferson 55402
Direct dial: (555) 555-8706
fmartin@martinlaw.com

January 17, 2011

Mr. Mike Carrington
Carrington Display, Inc.
1800 Elmwood Avenue
Davenport, Jefferson 55412

Re: Matthew Bryson's claims against Carrington Display, Inc.

Dear Mr. Carrington:

This firm represents Matthew Bryson, a salesperson in the Carrington Display Davenport office. Your company, Carrington Display, retaliated against Mr. Bryson because of an employment discrimination charge filed by his sister. This retaliation is illegal under the Civil Rights Act of 1964. Mr. Bryson is willing to settle his claims against Carrington Display for $150,000 if you accept this offer by January 28.

As you know, Mr. Bryson is the brother of Jennifer Randall, who until recently worked in your Norcross office. Carrington Display discriminated against Mr. Bryson after his sister filed a charge of sex discrimination against Carrington Display with the EEOC.

Before the filing of Ms. Randall's discrimination charge, Mr. Bryson was a successful salesperson for Carrington Display. Mr. Bryson has worked for the company since 2003. Between 2004 and 2009, Mr. Bryson received salesperson of the month awards at least once each year. While Mr. Bryson's sales grew each year based in part on his own efforts, he was also able to increase his client portfolio because of referrals he received from you.

Since you became aware of Ms. Randall's discrimination charge in January of 2010, Mr. Bryson's referrals have dried up. This is not based on a slowdown in the company's business. Other salespeople in the office continue to receive referrals from you. In the past, Mr. Bryson received his fair share of these referrals. Now he receives referrals only for labor-intensive, low-dollar sales. This cut in Mr. Bryson's referrals has negatively affected his income.

Title VII of the Civil Acts Right of 1964 prohibits an employer from retaliating against an employee because he has opposed an unlawful employment practice or because he has participated in any manner in an investigation of an unlawful employment practice. By cutting Mr. Bryson's referrals because of his sister's charge of sex discrimination, Carrington Display has violated Title VII.

Mr. Bryson is eager to put this matter behind him. He wants to continue as a fully producing member of the Carrington Display sales team—one who receives his fair share of potential clients. He also wants compensation for the income he has lost due to the decrease in his referrals over the past year. Under the law he is entitled to recover his attorneys' fees in this case. At this time, Mr. Bryson is willing to settle this dispute for a payment of $150,000 and an agreed permanent injunction requiring Carrington Display to allocate referrals to Mr. Bryson on an equal basis with the other salespeople.

Mr. Bryson's losses from the decreased referrals continue to mount. His attorneys' fees will, of course, also increase if we are forced to file suit to resolve this matter. Therefore, this offer to settle is open only until January 28. We hope to hear from you by then.

Sincerely,

Frederick Martin

Frederick Martin
For the Firm

C. SAMPLE COMPLAINT

United States District Court
For the Northern District of Jefferson

Matthew Bryson, Plaintiff v. **Carrington Display, Inc.,** Defendant	**Civil Action No.** _____

Plaintiff's Original Complaint

Introduction

1.   Mathew Bryson brings this action against Carrington Display, Inc., under Title VII of the Civil Rights Act of 1964, 42 U.S.C. §§ 2000e *et seq.* Carrington Display retaliated against Bryson because he opposed discriminatory actions against his sister, Jennifer Randall, by Carrington Display.

Parties

2.   Plaintiff, Bryson, is an adult citizen of the United States living in Davenport, Jefferson. Bryson is a white male. He is the brother of Jennifer Randall, a white female.

3.   Defendant, Carrington Display, is a company incorporated and doing business in Jefferson. During all times mentioned in this action, Carrington Display employed more than 15 employees and was an employer within the meaning of Title VII. Carrington Display may be served with process by serving its president and chief executive officer, Mike Carrington, at Carrington Display's offices:

Mike Carrington

1800 Elmwood Avenue

Davenport, Jefferson 55412.

1

Jurisdiction and Venue

4.   This court has federal-question jurisdiction over this suit under 28 U.S.C. § 1331 because this action arises under federal law, specifically 42 U.S.C. §§ 2000e et seq.

5.   This court has personal jurisdiction over Carrington Display because Carrington Display is incorporated in Jefferson and regularly conducts business in Jefferson. The acts creating the cause of action asserted in this lawsuit occurred in Jefferson.

6.   Venue is proper in this district under 28 U.S.C. § 1391(b) and (c) because a substantial part of the events giving rise to the claim occurred in this district and because Carrington Display is subject to personal jurisdiction in this district.

Exhaustion of Remedies

7.   Bryson has complied with all procedural requisites to this suit and has exhausted his administrative remedies. He has been issued a right-to-sue notice by the proper administrative agencies.

Facts

8.   Carrington Display designs, produces, and sells exhibit modules for use at trade shows.

9.   Bryson has been employed by Carrington Display since 2003. He is a successful salesperson. He has a large client portfolio and won salesperson of the month awards at least once each year in the years 2004 through 2009.

10.   Bryson generates many of his own sales leads from repeat clients, referrals from existing clients, and his own sales efforts. Before January 2010, Bryson also received numerous sales referrals from Carrington's president, Mike Carrington. These referrals were the result of calls to Carrington Display generated by the company's advertising and website, as well as sales leads

2

generated by other employees who were too busy to follow up with the potential clients.

11.   Bryson is paid on a commission basis, based on a percentage of the value of the sales he closes.

12.   In 2008, Bryson's sister, Jennifer Randall, was hired to work in Carrington Display's Norcross office. Randall was the only female employee in the Norcross office. Although she was hired as a salesperson, Randall was assigned tasks not given to other salespeople, including making coffee, preparing the showroom for client meetings, and answering phone calls that rolled over from other employees' phones. Randall believed that these administrative assignments interfered with her ability to perform her sales responsibilities.

13.   Randall attempted to resolve the inequality in her assignments through complaints to her supervisor. When her repeated complaints went unanswered, she filed a charge of sex discrimination with the EEOC in December 2009. Carrington Display became aware of this charge in January 2010.

14.   Mike Carrington criticized Randall's EEOC charge in Bryson's presence in January 2010. From Bryson's refusal to join in the criticism, Carrington discerned that Bryson supported his sister's claim and opposed Carrington Display's discriminatory actions against Randall.

15.   After that, the number of sales referrals that Bryson received from Carrington dropped. The referrals that Bryson did receive were for clients seeking lower-dollar items.

16.   The reduction in Bryson's referrals has negatively affected his income. If Carrington Display had not cut Bryson's referrals, Bryson would have closed more sales, and thus earned more income, in each month since January 2010.

3

Retaliation Claim

17.   Paragraphs 8 through 16 are incorporated in this claim.

18.   Carrington Display reduced the number of referrals given to Bryson in retaliation for the charge of sex discrimination filed by his sister and Bryson's support of that charge. This constitutes an unlawful employment practice under 42 U.S.C. § 2000e-3.

Jury Demand

19.   Plaintiff seeks a trial by jury of all issues in this case.

Prayer for Relief

Plaintiff Matthew Bryson seeks judgment against Defendant Carrington Display, Inc., including:

a.   An award of damages to compensate Bryson for income lost due to the decreased referrals in an amount this Court considers just, reasonable, and fair;

b.   An award of attorneys' fees and the costs of this action;

c.   An injunction requiring Carrington Display to distribute a fair share of referrals to Bryson; and

d.   Any other relief this Court deems appropriate.

Dated: February 21, 2011

Respectfully submitted,

Frederick Martin

Frederick Martin
Martin & Associates P.C.
1250 Monroe Street, Suite 311
Davenport, Jefferson 55402
fmartin@martinlaw.com
(555) 555-8706

4

D. SAMPLE ANSWER

United States District Court
For the Northern District of Jefferson

Matthew Bryson,
   Plaintiff

v.

Carrington Display, Inc.,
   Defendant

Civil Action No. 11-CV-743

Defendant Carrington Display's Answer

Carrington Display, Inc., Defendant, responds as follows to the allegations in Plaintiff's Original Complaint.

1.   Carrington Display denies the allegations in paragraph 1 of the Complaint.

2.   Carrington Display admits the allegations in paragraph 2 of the Complaint.

3.   Carrington Display admits the allegations in paragraph 3 of the Complaint.

4.   Carrington Display admits this Court has federal-question jurisdiction over this suit.

5.   Carrington Display admits this Court has personal jurisdiction over Carrington Display.

6.   Carrington Display admits venue is proper in this district.

7.   Carrington Display admits the allegations in paragraph 7 of the Complaint.

8.   Carrington Display admits the allegations in paragraph 8 of the Complaint.

9.   Carrington Display admits that Bryson has been employed by Carrington Display since 2003 and admits that he won salesperson of the month

1

awards at least once each year from 2004 to 2009. Carrington Display denies the remaining allegations in paragraph 9 of the Complaint.

10. Carrington Display admits that Bryson generates many of his own sales leads, that he has received (and continues to receive) numerous sales referrals from Mike Carrington, and that these referrals are generated from a number of sources. Carrington Display denies the remaining allegations in paragraph 10 of the Complaint.

11. Carrington Display admits the allegations in paragraph 11 of the Complaint.

12. Carrington Display admits that Bryson's sister, Jennifer Randall, was hired to work in Carrington Display's Norcross office in 2008. Carrington Display admits that Randall was the only female employee in the Norcross office. Carrington Display denies the remaining allegations in paragraph 12 of the Complaint.

13. Carrington Display admits that Randall filed a charge of sex discrimination with the EEOC in December 2009 and that it became aware of this charge in January 2010. Carrington Display denies the remaining allegations in paragraph 13 of the Complaint.

14. Carrington Display denies the allegations in paragraph 14 of the Complaint.

15. Carrington Display denies the allegations in paragraph 15 of the Complaint.

16. Carrington Display denies the allegations in paragraph 16 of the Complaint.

17. Carrington Display reasserts its answers to paragraphs 8 through 16 of the Complaint.

18. Carrington Display denies the allegations in paragraph 18 of the Complaint.

2

19. Carrington Display does not consent to the trial by jury of any issue not required by law to be tried by a jury, including but not limited to any determination of equitable remedies.

20. Carrington Display denies that Plaintiff is entitled to any relief sought in the Prayer for Relief of the Complaint.

Prayer for Relief

Defendant Carrington Display, Inc., prays that the Court deny Plaintiff Matthew Bryson the relief requested in the Complaint and grant Defendant such relief to which it may show itself justly entitled.

Dated: March 11, 2011

Respectfully submitted,

Eva Richards

Eva Richards
BISSELL & FORRESTER, LLP
Attorneys for Defendant
1000 Poplar Avenue, Suite 200
Davenport, Jefferson 55402
erichards@bissellforrester.com
(555) 555-1000

CERTIFICATE OF SERVICE

I certify that a true copy of this Defendant's Original Answer was served on:

Frederick Martin
Martin & Associates P.C.
1250 Monroe Street, Suite 311
Davenport, Jefferson 55402

by certified mail, return receipt requested, on March 11, 2011.

Eva Richards

Eva Richards

3

E. Sample Client Letter

Martin & Associates P.C.

1250 Monroe Street, Suite 311
Davenport, Jefferson 55402
Direct dial: (555) 555-8706
fmartin@martinlaw.com

June 17, 2011

Mr. Matthew Bryson
4307 Ridgewood Dr.
Davenport, Jefferson 55408

Re: Deposition of Mike Carrington in *Bryson v. Carrington Display, Inc.*;
Civil Action No. 11-CV-743; United States District Court for the
Northern District of Jefferson

Dear Matt:

This letter summarizes the impact of Mike Carrington's testimony at his deposition last week. His testimony will help us prove part of your claim for retaliation, but we still need more evidence about the action Carrington Display took against you. I've also enclosed a copy of the transcript of the deposition. I'll explain at the end of the letter what I would like you to do with the transcript within the next week.

As you know, your lawsuit claims that Carrington Display retaliated against you because of the charge of sex discrimination your sister filed with the EEOC. To prove your claim, we will need to show that

(1) you engaged in what is called "protected opposition" under the law;

(2) Carrington Display was aware of your opposition;

(3) Carrington Display took what is called an "adverse action" against you; and

(4) Carrington Display took that adverse action because of your protected opposition.

Mr. Carrington's testimony helps us the most on the first and second requirements. We'll need additional evidence on the third and fourth requirements.

On the first requirement, the court will have to decide whether you engaged in protected opposition. We have two possible arguments here. First, we'll argue that Jennifer's EEOC charge should "count" for you. In other words,

---

we'll argue that Carrington Display shouldn't be able to punish one of Jennifer's family members because of her EEOC charge. Some legal authority supports us on this position, but some courts have said the person filing the retaliation claim has to be the same person who engaged in the protected opposition. Second, we'll argue that because you were opposed to how Carrington Display was treating Jennifer, you meet this requirement.

The good news on the first requirement is that Mr. Carrington acknowledged mentioning Jennifer's charge during the January 2010 sales meeting you have described to me. At first he just said that you were silent about the charge and that he didn't expect you to say anything. When I pressed him, however, he conceded that other employees were making cracks criticizing Jennifer's charge and that you seemed to get annoyed. This will help us show that you opposed Carrington's treatment of Jennifer and that you supported her charge.

On the second requirement, Carrington Display's awareness, Mr. Carrington's testimony will help show that Carrington Display was aware of your opposition. If the court decides that Jennifer's charge can be treated as your protected activity, Mr. Carrington's testimony proves that Carrington Display was aware of her charge. Likewise, if the court decides that your silent opposition to Jennifer's treatment is sufficient, we can now show that Carrington Display was aware of that as well.

The third requirement, adverse action, presents the greatest challenge for us in gathering evidence. Our assertion is that by cutting your referrals, Carrington Display took an adverse action against you. The problem is that Mr. Carrington denies cutting your referrals. He also says there is no system by which he records or tracks referrals. If that's true, it will be difficult for us to show that your referrals have been reduced. Of course, you can testify that your referrals have been cut, but it isn't clear whether a court will find that to be enough evidence.

For the fourth requirement, that Carrington Display took the adverse action because of your protected opposition, we need to show that Carrington Display reduced your referrals because you opposed Jennifer's treatment. If we can show that the referrals dropped sharply in January 2010, the timing should help prove the connection. You can also testify about the comments Mr. Carrington made when giving referrals to your colleagues, which may help show the retaliatory motive against you.

My biggest concern at this point is coming up with enough evidence to show that your referrals were cut. I need your help on that. Please read Mr. Carrington's deposition. For each of his statements about how referrals come in to the office, how he distributes them, and how they are recorded, think carefully about who else would know about that and what records might exist about it. I want to meet with you next week to discuss where we should look next in our hunt for evidence of the cut in your referrals.

Please call me after you have read Mr. Carrington's deposition, and feel free to call before then if you have any questions.

Sincerely,

Frederick Martin

Frederick Martin
For the Firm

Enclosure: Transcript of Mike Carrington's deposition

F. Sample Interrogatories

United States District Court
For the Northern District of Jefferson

Matthew Bryson, Plaintiff	**Civil Action No. 11-CV-743**
v.	
Carrington Display, Inc., Defendant	

Defendant Carrington Display's Interrogatories to Matthew Bryson

To: Matthew Bryson, through his attorney Frederick Martin

Instructions

You must answer each of the following interrogatories separately and fully in writing under oath. If you object to any interrogatory, the grounds for objecting must be stated with specificity. The person who answers these interrogatories must sign them, and the attorney who objects must sign any objections.

You must serve your answers within 30 days of being served with these interrogatories. After you have responded to these interrogatories, you must supplement or correct your responses in a timely manner if you learn that in some material respect the response is incomplete or incorrect and if the additional or corrective information has not otherwise been made known to the other parties during the discovery process or in writing.

Definitions

1.   The terms "you" and "your" refer to Matthew Bryson.

2.   The term "identify" with respect to a person means to state the person's name, address, and telephone number.

1

---

3.   The term "identify" with respect to a client means to state the client's name, address, telephone number, and contact person.

Interrogatories

1.   Identify each person who participated in answering these interrogatories.

Answer:

2.   Describe your educational background, starting with high school, listing the name and address of each school you attended, the dates of your attendance, and any diplomas or degrees you received.

Answer:

3.   Identify each job you have held since graduating from high school, listing your employer, your position, your immediate supervisor, your responsibilities, your annual wages, and the dates of your employment.

Answer:

4.   Identify any crimes of which you have been convicted, listing the offense, the date of conviction, the location of the conviction, the punishment or penalty imposed for the conviction, and the date the punishment or penalty was completed or paid.

Answer:

5.   Identify each person with whom you have discussed Jennifer Randall's charge of discrimination against Carrington Display.

Answer:

6.   Describe each communication you have had with Mike Carrington regarding Jennifer Randall's charge of discrimination, identifying the date of the communication, the form of the communication (oral or written), other people who heard the communication or received a written copy of the communication, and the content of the communication.

2

Answer:

7.   Describe each unlawful employment practice you contend Carrington Display engaged in toward Jennifer Randall, identifying the date of the practice, the action taken, any witnesses to the practice, the discriminatory nature of the practice, and the persons who engaged in the practice.

Answer:

8.   Describe each action you took to oppose an unlawful employment practice by Carrington Display, identifying the date of the action, the action taken, any witnesses to the action, and the effect of the opposition.

Answer:

9.   Describe each charge you have made under Title VII of the Civil Rights Act of 1964, identifying when the charge was made, with what agency the charge was made, and what unlawful employment action the charge asserted.

Answer:

10.   Describe all testimony you have given in an investigation, proceeding, or hearing under Title VII of the Civil Rights Act of 1964, identifying when the testimony was given; where the testimony was given; in what investigation, proceeding, or hearing the testimony was given; and all persons present when the testimony was given.

Answer:

11.   Describe all actions you have taken to assist in any manner in an investigation, proceeding, or hearing under Title VII of the Civil Rights Act of 1964, identifying the date the action was taken, a description of the action taken, and all persons present when the action was taken.

Answer:

12.   Describe all instances when you have participated in an investigation, proceeding, or hearing under Title VII of the Civil Rights Act of

3

1964, listing the date of the participation, a description of the action taken, and all persons present when the action was taken.

Answer:

13. Describe each statement made by any employee of Carrington Display that you contend supports your claim that Carrington Display retaliated against you, identifying the person making the statement, whether the statement was oral or written, the date the statement was made, and the persons to whom the statement was made.

Answer:

14. Identify each person you contend received a referral that should have been directed to you.

Answer:

15. List each referral that you contend you should have received but did not, identifying the client, the date the referral was made, the person to whom the referral was made, and the gross proceeds of any sale that resulted from the referral.

Answer:

16. State the gross amount of sales you contend you lost because of the alleged reduction in your referrals.

Answer:

Dated: April 15, 2011

Respectfully submitted,

Eva Richards

Eva Richards
BISSELL & FORRESTER, LLP
Attorneys for Defendant
1000 Poplar Avenue, Suite 200
Davenport, Jefferson 55402
erichards@bissellforrester.com
(555) 555-1000

4

CERTIFICATE OF SERVICE

I certify that a true copy of this Defendant Carrington Display's
Interrogatories to Matthew Bryson was served on:

Frederick Martin
Martin & Associates P.C.
1250 Monroe Street, Suite 311
Davenport, Jefferson 55402

by certified mail, return receipt requested, on April 15, 2011.

Eva Richards

Eva Richards

5

G. Sample Requests for Production

United States District Court
For the Northern District of Jefferson

Matthew Bryson,
    Plaintiff

Civil Action No. 11-CV-743

v.

Carrington Display, Inc.,
    Defendant

Plaintiff Matthew Bryson's Requests for Production to Defendant Carrington Display

To: Carrington Display, through its attorney Eva Richards

You are requested to produce and permit Matthew Bryson or his representative to inspect or copy the following items in your possession, custody, or control. The items should be produced

On   May 16, 2011, at 1 p.m.,

At: The offices of Frederick Martin
        1250 Monroe Street, Suite 311
        Davenport, Jefferson

or at such other time and place as the parties may agree.

Instructions

You must respond in writing to this request within 30 days after being served. For each category listed, your response must state that inspection and related activities will be permitted as requested or state an objection to the request, including the reasons. An objection to part of a request must specify the part and permit inspection of the rest. After you have responded to these requests, you must supplement or correct your responses in a timely manner if you learn that in some material respect the response is incomplete or incorrect and if the

1

additional or corrective information has not otherwise been made known to the other parties during the discovery process or in writing.

Definitions

1.   The terms "you" and "your" refer to Carrington Display and its officers, agents, and employees.

2.   The term "documents or electronically stored information" is used as defined in Federal Rule of Civil Procedure 34(a)(1)(A).

3.   The term "referral" means the process by which you direct a client or potential client to one of your salespeople to handle the client's business.

Requests

1.   Documents or electronically stored information regarding the number of referrals you made each month from 2003 to the present.

Response:

2.   Documents or electronically stored information reflecting your annual gross sales for 2003 to the present.

Response:

3.   Documents or electronically stored information reflecting your annual net sales for 2003 to the present.

Response:

4.   Documents or electronically stored information regarding the commissions paid to each of your salespeople monthly for 2003 to the present.

Response:

5.   Documents or electronically stored information regarding the process you use to decide how to refer clients or potential clients to salespeople.

Response:

2

6.   Documents or electronically stored information regarding the number of referrals you gave to each of your salespeople monthly from 2003 to the present.

Response:

7.   Documents or electronically stored information regarding whether any referral you made to a salesperson resulted in a sale, the amount of the sale, or the commission paid to the employee because of the sale.

Response:

8.   Documents or electronically stored information regarding the number of telephone calls, e-mails, or in-person visits from potential clients generated by your advertising monthly from 2003 to the present.

Response:

9.   Documents or electronically stored information regarding the number of telephone calls, e-mails, or in-person visits from potential clients generated by your website monthly from 2003 to the present.

Response:

10.   Documents or electronically stored information regarding any transfer of a client's business from one salesperson to another from 2003 to the present.

Response:

11.   Documents or electronically stored information reflecting when you became aware of Jennifer Randall's charge of discrimination filed with the EEOC.

Response:

12.   Documents or electronically stored information containing notes or minutes of the January 2010 sales meeting with employees in your Davenport office.

Response:

3

13. Audio or visual recordings of the January 2010 sales meeting with employees in your Davenport office.

Response:

14. Documents or electronically stored information reflecting your reaction or response to the filing of an EEOC charge by Jennifer Randall.

Response:

15. Documents dated or generated after January 1, 2010, containing the words "Jennifer," "Randall," "Matthew," or "Bryson," or referring in any other terms to Jennifer Randall or Matthew Bryson.

Response:

Dated: April 11, 2011

Respectfully submitted,

Frederick Martin

Frederick Martin
Martin & Associates P.C.
1250 Monroe Street, Suite 311
Davenport, Jefferson 55402
fmartin@martinlaw.com
(555) 555-8706

CERTIFICATE OF SERVICE

I certify that I served a true copy of Plaintiff's Requests for Production to Defendant Carrington Display on:

Eva Richards
BISSELL & FORRESTER, LLP
1000 Poplar Avenue, Suite 200
Davenport, Jefferson 55402

by certified mail, return receipt requested, on April 11, 2011.

Frederick Martin

Frederick Martin

4

H. Sample Requests for Admission

United States District Court
For the Northern District of Jefferson

Matthew Bryson,
  Plaintiff

Civil Action No. 11-CV-743

v.

Carrington Display, Inc.,
  Defendant

Plaintiff Matthew Bryson's Requests for Admission to Defendant Carrington Display

To: Carrington Display, through its attorney Eva Richards

Instructions

You are asked to admit the following matters. Under Federal Rule of Civil Procedure 36, you are required to serve your written responses to these Requests for Admission on counsel for Matthew Bryson within 30 days of being served with these requests. If you fail to respond within 30 days, each matter will be deemed admitted.

If you do not admit any of these matters, your response must specifically deny it or state in detail why you cannot truthfully admit or deny it. Any denial must fairly respond in good faith to the substance of the matter. If good faith requires that you qualify an answer or deny only a part of the matter, your answer must specify the part admitted and qualify or deny the rest. You may assert lack of knowledge or information as a reason for failing to admit or deny only if you have made a reasonable inquiry and the information you know or can readily obtain is insufficient to enable you to admit or deny.

1

Requests

1.   Matthew Bryson is employed as a salesperson in the Davenport office of Carrington Display, Inc.

Response:

2.   Matthew Bryson is the brother of Jennifer Randall.

Response:

3.   Carrington Display hired Jennifer Randall to work as a salesperson in the Norcross office of Carrington Display in 2008.

Response:

4.   Mike Carrington knew when Jennifer Randall was hired that she was Matthew Bryson's sister.

Response:

5.   Matthew Bryson recommended Jennifer Randall for her position as a salesperson with Carrington Display.

Response:

6.   Mike Carrington was aware of the close relationship between Matthew Bryson and Jennifer Randall.

Response:

7.   Jennifer Randall filed a charge of sex discrimination against Carrington Display with the Equal Employment Opportunity Commission in December 2009.

Response:

8.   Mike Carrington became aware of Jennifer Randall's charge of sex discrimination against Carrington Display in January 2010.

2

Response:

9.   Matthew Bryson opposed Carrington Display's discriminatory treatment of Jennifer Randall.

Response:

10.   Mike Carrington knew that Matthew Bryson opposed Carrington Display's discriminatory treatment of Jennifer Randall.

Response:

11.   Mike Carrington criticized Jennifer Randall's charge of discrimination at the Davenport office monthly sales meeting in January 2010.

Response:

12.   Matthew Bryson was present at the Davenport office January 2010 sales meeting.

Response:

13.   Matthew Bryson refused to join with other employees in criticizing Jennifer Randall's charge of discrimination at the Davenport office January 2010 sales meeting.

Response:

14.   Mike Carrington understood from Matthew Bryson's reaction to the criticism of Jennifer Randall's claim at the Davenport office January 2010 sales meeting that Matthew Bryson opposed Carrington Display's practices regarding Jennifer.

Response:

15.   After the Davenport office January 2010 sales meeting, Mike Carrington reduced the number of sales referrals that he gave to Matthew Bryson.

Response:

16.   Since the January 2010 sales meeting, Mike Carrington has given Matthew Bryson referrals only for lower dollar-value, labor-intensive sales.

Response:

3

17. Mike Carrington reduced the number of sales referrals that he gave to Matthew Bryson because Matthew Bryson opposed the discriminatory treatment of Jennifer Randall.

Response:

18. Matthew Bryson is paid on a commission basis.

Response:

19. Matthew Bryson's commissions are based on a percentage of the value of the sales he closes.

Response:

20. A reduction in Matthew Bryson's referrals reduces his income-earning potential.

Response:

21. Matthew Bryson has earned less income since January 2010 than he would have earned if his referrals had not been reduced.

Response:

Dated: April 11, 2011

Respectfully submitted,

Frederick Martin

Frederick Martin
Martin & Associates P.C.
1250 Monroe Street, Suite 311
Davenport, Jefferson 55402
fmartin@martinlaw.com
(555) 555-8706

CERTIFICATE OF SERVICE

I certify that I served a true copy of this Plaintiff's Requests for Admission to Defendant Carrington Display on:

Eva Richards
BISSELL & FORRESTER, LLP
1000 Poplar Avenue, Suite 200
Davenport, Jefferson 55402

by certified mail, return receipt requested, on April 11, 2011.

Frederick Martin

Frederick Martin

4

I. Sample Opposing Counsel Letter

Martin & Associates P.C.

1250 Monroe Street, Suite 311
Davenport, Jefferson 55402
Direct dial: (555) 555-8706
fmartin@martinlaw.com

June 4, 2011

Ms. Eva Richards
Bissell & Forrester, LLP
1000 Poplar Avenue, Suite 200
Davenport, Jefferson 55402

Re: Requests for Production in *Bryson v. Carrington Display, Inc.*;
Civil Action No. 11-CV-743; United States District Court for the
Northern District of Jefferson

Dear Eva:

We need to address one of Carrington Display's responses to Matthew Bryson's requests for production. I've called your office about this discovery a couple of times in the last week, but I haven't heard back from you. I'm writing now in the hope that we can resolve this matter without the need for court intervention.

Specifically, the request for production to which we need a response is Bryson's Request for Production No. 4. It asks for:

Documents or electronically stored information regarding the commissions paid to each of your salespeople monthly for 2003 to the present.

You objected to this request, stating that the information sought was irrelevant and that the request was overly broad and unduly burdensome.

First, let me address your relevance objection. This information is directly relevant to Mr. Bryson's claim. As you know, we believe that Carrington Display directed referrals away from Mr. Bryson and to other salespeople once Carrington Display learned of Jennifer Randall's charge of discrimination with the EEOC. We will use information regarding the commissions paid to each of your salespeople to demonstrate that once Carrington Display learned of Ms. Randall's complaint, the commissions paid to other salespeople increased at a steeper rate than the commissions paid to Mr. Bryson. The information is relevant to Mr. Bryson's claim of an adverse employment action against him and to the amount of his damages.

Second, let me address the assertion that the request is overly broad and unduly burdensome. The time frame covered by this request, which covers only the years when Mr. Bryson has been employed by Carrington Display, is not too broad. Collecting the records for less than a decade should not be too burdensome. If the objection to breadth and burden is related to the number of employees covered by the request, perhaps we can work out a compromise. If you would be willing to withdraw your objection and respond to the discovery by June 15, we would be willing to limit the request to the employees in the Davenport office.

Please let me know if this compromise is acceptable to you. If it is, I will draft an agreement revising Mr. Bryson's Request for Production and stating your agreement to withdraw your objection and respond by June 15. If this compromise isn't acceptable to you, I welcome your suggestions for other ways that we can resolve this matter. Either way, I need to hear from you so we can get this matter moving. If I haven't heard from you by June 10, I will be forced to file a motion to compel.

I look forward to working with you toward a resolution of this issue.

Sincerely,

Frederick Martin

Frederick Martin
For the Firm

J. Sample Administrative Motion

United States District Court
For the Northern District of Jefferson

Matthew Bryson, Plaintiff	**Civil Action No. 11-CV-743**
v.	
Carrington Display, Inc., Defendant	

Plaintiff Matthew Bryson's Uncontested Motion
for Continuance of Hearing

Plaintiff Matthew Bryson asks this court to continue the hearing on Defendant's Motion for Summary Judgment, currently scheduled for November 1, 2011.

Grounds for Motion

No attorney familiar with Bryson's case will be available to represent Bryson at a hearing on November 1 because Bryson's lawyer, Frederick Martin, and his two associates will be trying a case in another court beginning on October 31.

Defendant Carrington Display filed its Motion for Summary Judgment on September 29, 2011. Bryson filed his response on October 13, 2011. On October 17, 2011, the Court's clerk notified counsel that the Court had set a hearing on the motion for November 1, 2011.

Mr. Martin is set for trial in Adams County District Court in the case of Kendall Boyce v. Alpha Computing on October 31, 2011. Both parties have

1

announced ready for trial. The case is the first setting on Judge Addy's docket for October 31 and trial is expected to begin that day. The trial is expected to last for 10 business days.

Mr. Martin's two associates will both be assisting in the Kendall Boyce trial. As a result, no attorney familiar with Bryson's case will be available to attend the hearing on November 1 and represent Bryson. Attempting to have another attorney substitute as counsel for Bryson at this stage of the case would result in substantial expense and would prejudice Bryson's interests. Therefore, Bryson asks that the hearing on Defendant's Motion for Summary Judgment be continued to the first available hearing date after November 14, 2011. This continuance is not sought for prejudice or delay but so that justice may be served.

Evidence

This motion is supported by the affidavit of Frederick Martin, attached as Exhibit A.

Lack of Opposition

Eva Richards, counsel for Carrington Display, has stated that Carrington Display does not oppose this motion.

Relief Sought

Plaintiff Matthew Bryson prays that the Court grant his Motion for Continuance of Hearing, continue the hearing on Defendant's Motion for Summary Judgment to the first available setting after November 14, 2011, and grant such other relief to which he may show himself justly entitled.

2

Dated: October 17, 2011   Respectfully submitted,

Frederick Martin

Frederick Martin
Martin & Associates P.C.
1250 Monroe Street, Suite 311
Davenport, Jefferson 55402
fmartin@martinlaw.com
(555) 555-8706

CERTIFICATE OF SERVICE

I certify that I served a true copy of this Plaintiff Matthew Bryson's Uncontested Motion for Continuance on:

Eva Richards
BISSELL & FORRESTER, LLP
1000 Poplar Avenue, Suite 200
Davenport, Jefferson 55402

by certified mail, return receipt requested, on October 17, 2011.

Frederick Martin

Frederick Martin

3

K. Sample Substantive Motion

United States District Court
For the Northern District of Jefferson

Matthew Bryson,
  Plaintiff

v.

Carrington Display, Inc.,
  Defendant

Civil Action No. 11-CV-743

Defendant Carrington Display's Motion for Summary Judgment

Plaintiff Matthew Bryson cannot prove at least two elements of his claim of retaliation under Title VII of the Civil Rights Act of 1964. Therefore, Carrington Display is entitled to summary judgment against Bryson's claim.

Introduction

Summary judgment should be granted against Bryson's case. Bryson alleges that his employer, Carrington Display, retaliated against him because of a discrimination charge filed by his sister, who was also a Carrington Display employee. To present a prima facie case of retaliation, a plaintiff must prove, among other elements, that he engaged in protected activity under Title VII and that the employer took adverse action against him. *Kessler v. Westchester Co. Dept. of Soc. Servs.*, 461 F.3d 199, 205-06 (2d Cir. 2006). The evidence shows that while Bryson's sister engaged in protected activity, Bryson did not. The evidence also shows that Carrington Display did not take an adverse action against Bryson. Because Bryson cannot make out at least two elements of his claim, this Court should grant summary judgment against him.

1

Statement of Facts

Carrington Display designs, produces, and sells display modules for trade shows. (Aff. Mike Carrington (Sept. 27, 2011), attached as Exhibit A.) Bryson works as a salesman in Carrington Display's Davenport office. Carrington Display hired Bryson in 2003, and he remains employed there to this day. (*Id.*)

Carrington Display hired Bryson's sister, Jennifer Randall, to work in Carrington Display's Norcross office in 2008. (*Id.*) In December 2009, Randall filed a charge of discrimination against Carrington Display with the Equal Employment Opportunity Commission. (*Id.*) Bryson has not testified in Randall's proceeding against Carrington Display or assisted Randall with her claim. (Transcr. Depo. Matthew Bryson 15:3-17:8 (Aug. 29, 2011), attached as Exhibit B.) Bryson has not discussed his sister's discrimination charge with anyone at the company. (*Id.* at 25:14-26:20.)

Bryson generates sales through his own efforts and through sales referrals he receives from Mike Carrington, the president and CEO of Carrington Display. (Aff. Carrington.) Carrington directs sales referrals to salespeople when customers cold-call Carrington Display because of its advertising or reputation or when a salesperson will be unable to assist a client or potential client. (*Id.*) Carrington has sent sales referrals to Bryson throughout Bryson's term of employment. (*Id.*) Carrington has not at any time ceased sending sales referrals to Bryson. (*Id.*) Carrington does not believe that Bryson's referrals have decreased over time, although Carrington does not track referrals and therefore cannot verify the number of referrals over time. (*Id.*) Carrington Display does not count the number of calls it receives from potential customers, so it is possible that the overall number of available referrals has decreased since January 2010. (*Id.*)

2

Carrington Display does not have an organized system for making sales referrals to its salespeople. (*Id.*) President Mike Carrington makes the referrals based on a salesperson's availability and likely rapport with the potential customer. (*Id.*) Carrington attempts to equalize the referrals among his sales-people, but he does not guarantee that all salespeople will receive an equal number of referrals over any given time period. (*Id.*) His primary concern is customer satisfaction, not equalization of referrals. (*Id.*) He also attempts to direct referrals to salespeople who are having a slow sales period. (*Id.*) Furthermore, a referral does not necessarily result in a sale. In fact, less than one-third of all referrals result in a sale that closes. (*Id.*)

Bryson's total sales, and thus his income, increased in 2010 over the 2009 levels. (*Id.*; Aff. Norma Chavez (Sept. 27, 2011), attached as Exhibit C; Bryson's pay stubs for January 2009 through December 2010, attached as Exhibits C1-C24.) So far for 2011, his total sales and income have increased for the first half of the year over the 2010 levels. (Aff. Carrington; Aff. Chavez; Bryson's pay stubs for January 2010 through June 2010 and January 2011 through June 2011, attached as Exhibits C13-C18 and C25-C30.)

Motion Standard

Summary judgment should be granted if "the pleadings, the discovery and disclosure materials on file, and any affidavits show that there is no genuine issue as to any material fact and that the movant is entitled to judgment as a matter of law." Fed. R. Civ. P. 56(c). Rule 56(c) "mandates the entry of summary judgment, after adequate time for discovery and upon motion, against a party who fails to make a showing sufficient to establish the existence of an element essential to that party's case, and on which that party will bear the burden of proof at trial." *Celotex Corp. v. Catrett*, 477 U.S. 317, 322 (1986).

3

Argument and Authorities

Bryson is unable to make out a prima facie case of retaliation, making summary judgment against his claim appropriate. The retaliation prohibition in Title VII states:

> It shall be an unlawful employment practice for any employer to discriminate against any of his employees . . . because he has opposed any practice made an unlawful employment practice by this subchapter, or because he has made a charge, testified, assisted, or participated in any manner in an investigation, proceeding, or hearing under this subchapter.

42 U.S.C. § 2000e-3 (2006).

To present a prima facie case of retaliation under Title VII, a plaintiff must provide evidence sufficient to permit a rational trier of fact to find that:

(1)   he engaged in protected participation or opposition under Title VII;

(2)   the employer was aware of this activity;

(3)   the employer took adverse action against the plaintiff; and

(4)   a causal connection exists between the protected activity and the adverse action.

Kessler, 461 F.3d at 205-206. For purposes of this motion, Carrington Display challenges Bryson's ability to present evidence on the first and third elements of his prima facie case.

I.   Bryson has not engaged in protected participation or opposition under Title VII.

Summary judgment is appropriate because Bryson cannot prove the first element of his claim. Bryson has not opposed any practice made unlawful by Title VII, nor has he participated in any investigation, proceeding, or hearing under this subchapter. Section 2000e-3 prohibits discrimination against an employee only

4

if "he has opposed any practice made an unlawful employment practice by this subchapter, or because he has made a charge, testified, assisted, or participated in any manner in an investigation, proceeding, or hearing under this subchapter." 42 U.S.C. § 2000e-3(a). Bryson has not engaged in any such opposition or participation.

A.   Bryson has not opposed an unlawful employment practice.

Bryson has taken no action that constitutes opposition to an unlawful employment practice. The term "oppose" is not defined in the statute. Therefore, the term should be interpreted according to its ordinary meaning. *Crawford v. Metro. Govt. of Nashville*, 129 S. Ct. 846, 850 (2009). Communicating to the employer a belief that the employer has engaged in employment discrimination almost always constitutes opposition. *Id.* at 851. Taking a stand against an employer's discriminatory practices would also constitute opposition. *Id.* The Supreme Court decided that the opposition clause covered the statements plaintiff Vicky Crawford made to a human resources officer as part of an investigation into sexual harassment. *Id.*

In contrast to Crawford, Bryson has done nothing. He has not discussed his sister's claims with anyone at Carrington Display. He has not taken a stand against any alleged discriminatory practices. In short, he has taken no action that showed he "opposed" anything.

Bryson apparently wants his unexpressed distaste for Mike Carrington's conduct to count as opposition. This Court should not allow an employee to take no action in the face of alleged discriminatory conduct and later, with hindsight, assert that he was "opposed" to the conduct. Such a standard would allow any employee to assert that any employment action taken against him was in retaliation for some supposed opposition to the employer's conduct. As Justice Alito recognized in his concurrence in *Crawford*, "[a]n interpretation of the

5

opposition clause that protects conduct that is not active and purposive would have important practical implications." 129 S. Ct. at 854 (Alito, J., concurring). These implications could include acceleration in the number of retaliation claims filed. *Id.* at 855. Rather than allowing employees to assert retaliation claims when they have taken no action in opposition to an employer's conduct, this Court should require some activity demonstrating the employee's opposition. Bryson took no such action. Summary judgment against his claim is warranted.

B.   Bryson has not participated in any manner in his sister's Title VII proceeding.

In addition to taking no action to express opposition to alleged discriminatory practices, Bryson has not participated in his sister's Title VII charge. Under the retaliation provision, an employer may not discriminate against any of its employees "because he has made a charge, testified, assisted, or participated in any manner in an investigation, proceeding, or hearing under this subchapter." 42 U.S.C. § 2000e-3(a). The word "he" refers to the employee against whom the employer allegedly retaliates. Thus, that employee must be the one who has made a charge or participated in some manner in a proceeding under Title VII. Bryson concedes that he has not made a charge or participated in his sister's charge.

Instead, Bryson apparently relies on his sister's participation in a Title VII proceeding to satisfy the participation clause. The Second Circuit has not yet decided whether a claim exists under Title VII for third-party retaliation claims. *Thomas v. Am. Horse Shows Assoc.*, 205 F.3d 1324 (table), 2000 WL 232401 (2d Cir. 2000). Other circuits, however, have recognized that the plain language of the statute does not authorize a claim by a plaintiff who did not himself engage in protected activity. *E.g., Thompson v. N. Am. Stainless*, 567 F.3d 804, 809 (6th Cir. 2009) (affirming summary judgment against employee who was terminated

6

after his fiancée filed a sex discrimination charge against their employer); *Holt v. JTM Indus., Inc.*, 89 F.3d 1224, 1226-1227 (5th Cir. 1996) (holding that a plaintiff could not sue for retaliation under nearly identical language in the Age Discrimination in Employment Act simply because his spouse has engaged in protected activity). This Court should likewise follow the plain language of the statute and grant summary judgment against Bryson's claim because he has not participated in a Title VII proceeding.

II. Carrington Display has not taken an adverse action against Bryson.

Summary judgment is also appropriate because Bryson cannot prove the third element of his claim, that Carrington Display took an adverse action against him. To prove an adverse action, "a plaintiff must show that a reasonable employee would have found the challenged action materially adverse." *Burlington N. & Santa Fe Ry. v. White*, 548 U.S. 53, 68 (2006). The United States Supreme Court has emphasized that a retaliation claim requires a showing of "*material adversity,*" to "separate significant from trivial harms." *Id.* (emphasis in original). The court excludes from coverage the "petty slights or minor annoyances that often take place at work and that all employees experience." *Id.*

Burlington Northern illustrates the level of adversity necessary to prove an adverse action. To prove she experienced an adverse action, the plaintiff, White, offered evidence that she was reassigned to duties that were "more arduous and dirtier" and that her prior position was "objectively considered a better job." *Id.* at 71. White also showed that the employer's action forced White and her family to live for 37 days with no income. *Id.* at 72. The court found this evidence sufficient to show a material adverse action. *Id.* at 70. In contrast, the court noted that a supervisor's refusal to invite an employee to lunch is normally a trivial, nonactionable petty slight. *Id.* at 69.

7

In a case with facts analogous to those Bryson alleges, the Eighth Circuit affirmed a summary judgment against an employee who alleged that she was given inadequate help with her sales. *Devin v. Schwan's Home Serv., Inc.*, 491 F.3d 778, 781 (8th Cir. 2007). The employee, Jessica Devin, was a route manager for Schwan's, responsible for making deliveries, collecting payments, and soliciting customers. *Id.* Among other complaints, Devin alleged that she was not provided with a "route builder" on her route. *Id.* at 782. A route builder is a Schwan's employee who accompanies a route manager on her route, obtaining new customers by soliciting noncustomers. *Id.* While the record contained evidence of some value to having a route builder assigned to one's route, the court said Devin failed to show that route builders had significant value. *Id.* at 786. Establishing that a route builder can be beneficial did not meet Devin's burden of showing that denial of a route builder was a materially significant disadvantage. *Id.*

Bryson likewise cannot prove that he has suffered a material adverse action. Unlike White, his job duties were not changed and he was not forced to live without income. Indeed, his income has increased during the time period he alleges that Carrington Display has taken adverse action against him. Bryson claims that Carrington Display has given him fewer sales referrals over the last year and half, but he cannot quantify the decrease in referrals or identify any lost sales. Like Devin's showing about the value of route builders, Bryson can at best show that getting more sales referrals would be beneficial, but he cannot show a materially significant disadvantage based on a reduction in his referrals—which he also cannot prove. Because Bryson can prove only trivial harms and not material adversity, summary judgment should be granted against his claim.

8

Relief Sought

Defendant Carrington Display, Inc., prays that the Court grant this Motion for Summary Judgment, enter an order denying Plaintiff Matthew Bryson the relief requested in his Complaint, and grant Defendant such other relief to which it may show itself justly entitled.

Dated: September 29, 2011

Respectfully submitted,

Eva Richards
_____

Eva Richards
BISSELL & FORRESTER, LLP
Attorneys for Defendant
1000 Poplar Avenue, Suite 200
Davenport, Jefferson 55402
erichards@bissellforrester.com
(555) 555-1000

CERTIFICATE OF SERVICE

I certify that a true copy of this Defendant Carrington Display's Motion for Summary Judgment was served on:

Frederick Martin
Martin & Associates P.C.
1250 Monroe Street, Suite 311
Davenport, Jefferson 55402

by certified mail, return receipt requested, on September 29, 2011.

Eva Richards
_____

Eva Richards

9

L. Sample Response

United States District Court
For the Northern District of Jefferson

Matthew Bryson,
   Plaintiff

v.

Carrington Display, Inc.,
   Defendant

Civil Action No. 11-CV-743

Plaintiff Matthew Bryson's Response to Defendant Carrington Display's Motion for Summary Judgment

Plaintiff Matthew Bryson sued Carrington Display, Inc., for unlawful retaliation under Title VII of the Civil Rights Act of 1964. Carrington Display's unlawful retaliation consists of punishing Bryson because of his sister's claim of sex discrimination against Carrington Display and his support of her claim. Contrary to the assertions in Defendant's Motion for Summary Judgment, Bryson can make out a prima facie claim of illegal retaliation.

Introduction

Matthew Bryson and his sister, Jennifer Randall, both worked as salespeople for Carrington Display. Carrington Display allegedly discriminated against Randall on the basis of her sex. When Randall's complaints within the company proved futile, she filed a charge of sex discrimination with the Equal Employment Opportunity Commission. After Randall filed her charge, Carrington Display retaliated against her brother, slashing the number of referrals that Bryson was given.

Bryson can prove all elements of his retaliation claim. Carrington's summary judgment motion asserts that Bryson cannot prove that (1) he engaged

1

in protected opposition or participation and (2) he suffered an adverse action. Bryson offers enough evidence to create an issue of fact on both elements. Summary judgment should be denied.

Statement of Facts

Bryson has worked as a salesperson for Carrington Display since 2003. (Aff. Matthew Bryson (Oct. 10, 2011), attached as Exhibit A.) Bryson has been a successful salesperson, earning "salesperson of the month" awards at least once a year from 2004 through 2009. (*Id.*) From 2003 until January 2010, Bryson received numerous sales referrals from Carrington Display's president, Mike Carrington. (*Id.*) Approximately one-third of these referrals led to sales. (*Id.*) Because Bryson is paid on a commission basis, the sales referrals led to a direct increase in Bryson's income. (*Id.*)

Carrington Display hired Bryson's sister, Randall, in 2008. (*Id.*) Randall worked in an office in which she was the only female employee. (Aff. Jennifer Randall (Oct. 11, 2011), attached as Exhibit B.) Although Randall was hired as a salesperson, Carrington Display assigned her duties not given to the male salespeople, such as making coffee and answering phones. (*Id.*) These additional duties interfered with Randall's ability to make sales. (*Id.*) Randall complained to her supervisors about these inequities, but the supervisors failed to address them. (*Id.*) In December 2009, Randall filed a charge of discrimination with the EEOC against Carrington Display. (*Id.*) Carrington Display was informed of this charge in January 2010. (Transcr. Depo. Mike Carrington 27:13-28:1 (Sept. 2, 2011), attached as Exhibit C.)

At the January 2010 monthly sales meeting, Mike Carrington made a derogatory reference to Randall's claim. (Aff. Bryson.) Several employees joined in the criticism of the claim. (*Id.*) One employee said, "You are better off not to hire a woman in the first place." (*Id.*) Another said, "Mike, you ought to know that

2

if you get involved with a woman, the lawyers are never far behind." (*Id.*) Bryson supported his sister's charge and thought Carrington had discriminated against her. (*Id.*) When Mike Carrington and other employees made comments critical of her charge, Bryson was furious. (*Id.*) He could feel his cheeks turning bright red. (*Id.*) Carrington admits that employees made derogatory comments about Randall's claim during this meeting. (Transcr. Depo. Carrington 53:6–53:8.) Carrington also admits that he could tell Bryson was annoyed by the criticism. (*Id.*)

After this sales meeting, Carrington cut the number of sales referrals he gave to Bryson each month. (Aff. Bryson.) While Bryson had previously received several referrals every month, months now pass in which Bryson receives no referrals. (*Id.*) The few referrals he does receive are for labor-intensive but small dollar-value orders. (*Id.*) While Bryson has managed to increase his income over the past year and a half through his own sales efforts, his income would have been higher if Carrington Display had not cut his referrals. (*Id.*)

Bryson has overheard comments demonstrating that Carrington intentionally reduced the number of referrals he gave to Bryson to punish Bryson for the charge of discrimination filed by Randall. (*Id.*) On one occasion, Bryson heard Carrington tell another salesperson that he was giving the salesperson the referral because the customer would appreciate having a "real man" on the job. (*Id.*) On another occasion Carrington told Bryson he would not send a customer to him because the customer "wouldn't want to deal with a complainer." (*Id.*)

Motion Standard

A plaintiff, to defeat a defendant's motion for summary judgment, need only present evidence from which a jury might return a verdict in his favor. *Anderson v. Liberty Lobby, Inc.*, 477 U.S. 242, 257 (1986). If he does so, there is a genuine issue of fact that requires a trial. *Id.* The court must resolve all ambiguities and draw all inferences in the nonmoving party's favor. *Graham v. Long Island R.R.*,

3

230 F.3d 34, 38 (2d Cir. 2000). The trial court's role at this stage is "to identify issues to be tried, not decide them." *Id.*

Argument and Authorities

Summary judgment should be denied because a jury could return a verdict in Bryson's favor on his retaliation claim. Section 2000e-3 of United States Code title 42 prohibits employers from retaliating to prevent employees from exercising their rights under the Civil Rights Act of 1964. 42 U.S.C. § 2000e-3 (2006); *see generally Deravin v. Kerik*, 335 F.3d 195, 203 (2d Cir. 2003). Section 2000e-3 states:

> It shall be an unlawful employment practice for any employer to discriminate against any of his employees . . . because he has opposed any practice made an unlawful employment practice by this subchapter, or because he has made a charge, testified, assisted, or participated in any manner in an investigation, proceeding, or hearing under this subchapter.

42 U.S.C. § 2000e-3. The Second Circuit has recognized that "Title VII's anti-retaliation provision is broadly drawn." *Deravin*, 335 F.3d at 203. Indeed, the Second Circuit has described this provision as "expansive" and said that it "seemingly contains no limitations." *Id.*

Bryson can prove that—at a minimum—a genuine issue of material fact exists as to both elements that Carrington Display challenges. Specifically, Bryson can show that there is a fact issue about whether he engaged in protected opposition or participation and whether Carrington Display took adverse action against him.

I.   Bryson has engaged in protected opposition or participation under Title VII.

Bryson's actions are sufficient to raise a fact issue about whether he has engaged in protected opposition or participation under Title VII. Title VII's anti-retaliation provision has two clauses. *Crawford v. Metro. Govt. of*

4

Nashville, 129 S. Ct. 846, 850 (2009). The "opposition clause" makes it unlawful to discriminate against an employee because he has opposed a practice made unlawful by Title VII. *Id.* The "participation clause" makes it unlawful to discriminate against an employee because he has participated in any manner in a proceeding under Title VII. *Id.* A fact issue exists about whether Bryson satisfies the opposition clause. This Court should decide as a matter of law that Bryson's sister's charge of sex discrimination satisfies the participation clause for Bryson's claim.

A.   A genuine issue of fact exists about whether Bryson satisfies the opposition clause.

Bryson's demonstrated hostility to the sexual discrimination against his sister is sufficient for a reasonable jury to find that he has satisfied the opposition clause. Because the term "oppose" is not defined in Title VII, the term carries its ordinary meaning. *Id.* In *Crawford* the Supreme Court quoted this definition of "oppose": "to be hostile or adverse to, as in opinion." *Id.* (quoting Random House Dictionary of the English Language 1359 (2d ed. 1987)).

In reversing a Sixth Circuit decision that required "active, consistent 'opposing' activities," the Supreme Court said: "'Oppose' goes beyond 'active, consistent' behavior in ordinary discourse, where we would naturally use the word to speak of someone who has taken no action at all to advance a position beyond disclosing it." *Id.* at 851. The Court offered as an example people who "oppose" capital punishment even if they do not write public letters, take to the streets, or resist the government. *Id.*

A jury could find that Bryson opposed Carrington Display's treatment of his sister. He was "hostile" and "adverse" to the discrimination against her. A jury could also find that Bryson disclosed this position when he refused to join in the criticism of Randall's claim and reacted visibly in the face of it. Indeed, Carrington has conceded that he could tell that Bryson was annoyed by the criticism of his sister's claim.

5

The opposition clause does not contain an action requirement. It states only that one must have "opposed" a practice. 42 U.S.C. § 2000e-3. Therefore Carrington Display's argument that Bryson was required to take some action to demonstrate his opposition is misplaced. (Def.'s Mot. S.J. 5 (Sept. 29, 2011)). The opposition clause can be contrasted with the participation clause, which requires that one make a charge, testify, assist, or participate in a proceeding or investigation. 42 U.S.C. § 2000e-3. No such activities are listed in the opposition clause. Because no certain action is required to oppose a practice, and because Bryson disclosed his opinion about the discriminatory treatment of his sister to his employer, a jury could find that Bryson satisfies the opposition clause.

B.   Randall's charge of sex discrimination can satisfy the participation requirement for Bryson's retaliation claim.

Summary judgment is also inappropriate because Randall's discrimination charge can form the basis of Bryson's retaliation claim. Holding to the contrary would allow employers to circumvent the anti-retaliation provision of Title VII by retaliating against an employee's family member.

The better-reasoned authorities recognize that third-party retaliation claims should be allowed under Title VII. The Second Circuit has not yet addressed the issue. *Thomas v. Am. Horse Shows Assoc.*, 205 F.3d 1324 (table), 2000 WL 232401 (2d Cir. 2000). But the EEOC has. In its Compliance Manual, the EEOC states that Title VII prohibits "retaliation against someone so closely related to or associated with the person exercising his or her statutory rights that it would discourage or prevent the person from pursuing those rights." EEOC Compliance Manual § 8-2(C)(3) (Westlaw current through Aug. 2009). In an example, the EEOC said it would be unlawful for an employer to retaliate against an employee because his spouse filed an EEOC charge. *Id.* The EEOC

6

Compliance Manual is entitled to deference so long as it is persuasive. *Deravin*, 335 F.3d at 204 n. 7.

Another district court within the Second Circuit has recognized that disallowing third-party retaliation claims would "provide a means for an employer to circumvent Title VII's remedial scheme." *Gonzalez v. N.Y. State Dept. of Correctional Servs.*, 122 F. Supp. 2d 335, 347 (N.D.N.Y. 2000). The court in *Gonzalez* noted that interpreting section 2000e-3(a) to disallow a wife's claim for retaliation after her husband complained of discrimination would contravene Title VII's enforcement provisions. *Id.* "Title VII should not be construed so narrowly." *Id.*

While Carrington Display correctly cites two circuit court opinions that have, indeed, construed Title VII so narrowly, both cases drew dissents on this basis. *See Thompson v. N. Am. Stainless*, 567 F.3d 804 (6th Cir. 2009) (Moore, J., dissenting, and Martin, J., dissenting); *Holt v. JTM Indus., Inc.*, 89 F.3d 1224 (5th Cir. 1996) (Dennis, J., dissenting). As Justice Dennis noted, "the literal meaning of the anti-retaliation provision should not be used to undermine the clear purpose and intent" of the statute. *Holt*, 89 F.3d at 1231 (Dennis, J., dissenting).

The EEOC's guidance—allowing for third-party claims—is persuasive and should be followed. This Court should find that Randall's charge of discrimination can serve as the basis for Bryson's retaliation claim as a matter of law, satisfying the participation clause on Bryson's behalf.

II. A fact issue exists about whether Carrington Display took adverse action against Bryson.

Bryson's evidence also raises a fact issue about whether Carrington Display has taken an adverse action against him. To show an adverse action, "a plaintiff must show that a reasonable employee would have found the challenged action materially

7

adverse, which in this context means it well might have dissuaded a reasonable worker from making or supporting a charge of discrimination." *Burlington N. & Santa Fe Ry. v. White*, 548 U.S. 53, 68 (2006) (internal citations omitted). Summary judgment is inappropriate where the plaintiff adduces evidence sufficient to create a genuine issue of fact as to whether changes in his employment were materially adverse. *Kessler v. Westchester Co. Dept. of Social Servs.*, 461 F.3d 199, 201 (2d Cir. 2006).

In holding that there was a sufficient evidentiary basis to support the plaintiff's claim of an adverse action in *Burlington*, the Court noted that the plaintiff, White, was reassigned from job duties that were desirable to job duties that were less desirable. 548 U.S. at 71. Rejecting the defendant's argument that a reassignment of duties could not constitute retaliatory discrimination, the Court said, "[c]ommon sense suggests that one good way to discourage an employee such as White from bringing discrimination charges would be to insist that she spend more time performing the more arduous duties and less time performing those that are easier or more agreeable." *Id.* at 70–71.

Similarly, the Second Circuit reversed a summary judgment against an employee's retaliation claim where the employee's evidence showed that his duties were reduced. *Kessler*, 461 F.3d at 210. The employee was transferred, but the transfer did not affect his job title, job grade, salary, benefits, or hours of work. *Id.* at 202. Nevertheless, the Second Circuit concluded that the employee presented evidence sufficient to create a fact issue on whether the reassignment to which he was subjected could dissuade a reasonable employee in his position from complaining of unlawful discrimination. *Id.* at 209.

Kessler can be contrasted with the Eighth Circuit case on which Carrington Display relies, *Devin v. Schwan's Home Service, Inc.*, 491 F.3d 778 (8th Cir. 2007). The Eighth Circuit confirmed summary judgment for the employer after

8

the plaintiff alleged numerous forms of adverse treatment but failed to produce evidence showing significant harm. *Id.* at 788. The plaintiff alleged that she was deprived of a route builder to help her increase her sales, but proved only that it "can be" beneficial to have a route builder. *Id.* at 786. Because of this evidentiary failure, the Eighth Circuit affirmed summary judgment against her claims. *Id.* at 790.

Like the plaintiffs in *Burlington Northern and Kessler*, Bryson has offered sufficient evidence for a jury to conclude that Carrington Display has taken an adverse action against him. A salesperson, especially one paid on a commission basis, obviously does not want to lose sales referrals. Depriving Bryson of referrals makes his job harder, just like White's employer made her job harder by assigning her more arduous duties. Just as the reassignment of Kessler could dissuade a reasonable employee from supporting a charge of discrimination, a reasonable employee in Bryson's position might well be dissuaded from making or supporting a charge of discrimination if he knew that his employer would cut his referrals.

Finally, Bryson's evidence does not suffer from the deficiencies that defeated the plaintiff's claims in *Devin*. While Devin failed to show a significant harm from being deprived of a route builder, Bryson's evidence shows that about one-third of referrals turn into sales. Because Bryson is compensated on a commission basis, each lost sale is a reduction in his potential income. Because Bryson's referrals have been cut from several each month to few—and sometimes none—each month, his earning potential has been reduced. A jury could decide that such a reduction might well dissuade a reasonable employee from supporting a charge of discrimination. Thus, Bryson's evidence raises a fact issue on the adverse action element of his claim, making summary judgment inappropriate.

9

Relief Sought

Plaintiff Matthew Bryson prays that the Court deny Defendant's Motion for Summary Judgment and grant such other relief to which he may show himself justly entitled.

Dated: October 13, 2011

Respectfully submitted,

Frederick Martin

Frederick Martin
Martin & Associates P.C
1250 Monroe Street, Suite 311
Davenport, Jefferson 55402
fmartin@martinlaw.com
(555) 555-8706

CERTIFICATE OF SERVICE

I certify that I served a true copy of this Plaintiff Matthew Bryson's Response to Defendant Carrington Display's Motion for Summary Judgment on:

Eva Richards
BISSELL & FORRESTER, LLP
1000 Poplar Avenue, Suite 200
Davenport, Jefferson 55402

by certified mail, return receipt requested, on October 13, 2011.

Frederick Martin

Frederick Martin

10

M. Sample Business Records Affidavit

United States District Court
For the Northern District of Jefferson

Matthew Bryson, Plaintiff v. **Carrington Display, Inc.,** Defendant	**Civil Action No. 11-CV-743**

**Affidavit of Norma Chavez In Support Of
Defendant's Motion for Summary Judgment**

State of Jefferson

County of Adams

My name is Norma Chavez. I am over the age of twenty one, have never been convicted of a felony, and am otherwise qualified to make this affidavit. I have personal knowledge of the facts stated in this affidavit.

I am the accountant for Carrington Display, Inc. The salespeople at Carrington Display are paid on a commission basis. I am responsible for calculating the amount paid to each salesperson each month. I base the calculation for each employee on the dollar value of sales generated by that employee that have closed that month. The dollar value of sales is multiplied by the commission percentage, which is the same for each employee and has not changed since 2005.

I prepare the pay checks and pay stubs for each employee. The pay stubs show the amount the employee was paid each month.

Exhibits C1 through C12 are true and correct copies of Matthew Bryson's pay stubs for January through December 2009. Exhibits C13 through C24 are true and correct copies of Bryson's pay stubs for January through December 2010. Exhibits C25 through C30 are true and correct copies of Bryson's pay stubs for January through June 2011. I made Exhibits C1 through C30 in the regular course of Carrington Display's business. It is the regular course of business for Carrington Display to make such records at the time of the transactions reflected on them.

Norma Chavez
Norma Chavez

1

Signed and sworn before me, a notary public for the state of Jefferson, on September 27, 2011.

Roxanne Hill

Printed Name: Roxanne Hill
My commission expires: 11/2011

2

N. Sample Affidavit About Facts of the Case

United States District Court
For the Northern District of Jefferson

Matthew Bryson, Plaintiff	**Civil Action No. 11-CV-743**
v.	
Carrington Display, Inc., Defendant	

**Affidavit of Mike Carrington In Support Of
Defendant's Motion for Summary Judgment**

State of Jefferson

County of Adams

My name is Mike Carrington. I am over the age of twenty one, have never been convicted of a felony, and am otherwise qualified to make this affidavit. I have personal knowledge of the facts stated in this affidavit.

I am the president and chief executive officer of Carrington Display, Inc. Our company designs, produces, and sells exhibit modules for trade shows. As the president of Carrington Display, I oversee all the company's operations. Therefore, I am familiar with the employment of Matthew Bryson and Jennifer Randall. I am also familiar with the company's procedure for handling sales referrals.

Matthew Bryson has been employed as a salesman by Carrington Display, Inc., since 2003. He works in our Davenport office. His sister, Jennifer Randall, began working in our Norcross office in 2008. Ms. Randall filed a charge with the EEOC in December 2009, alleging that Carrington Display discriminated against her because she was female. Carrington Display has not discriminated against Ms. Randall, and we vigorously deny her charges. Her charge has not in any way affected how I treat Mr. Bryson or how any other employee of Carrington Display treats Mr. Bryson.

Our salespeople generate most of their own sales leads. At times, however, we get cold calls from customers, generated by our advertising, our website, or our company's strong reputation in the marketplace. All of these calls are directed to me or my secretary. I then farm these referrals out to the sales staff. I base my decisions about which salesperson to direct a call to on the salesperson's

1

availability and whether I think the particular salesperson could establish a good rapport with the potential customer.

I try to spread the referrals among our salespeople. However, I do not track the referrals or maintain an organized system to ensure that the referrals are evenly distributed. Attempting to ensure mathematical equivalence in the referrals would impede customer service because the salesperson whose "turn" it is for a referral might not be available at the time. Since customer service is our primary goal, finding a salesperson who will make the best match for the customer is my goal. I also try to direct referrals to employees who are having a slow month. Because I do not track these cold calls, I do not know whether the number of calls has increased or decreased in the last two years.

Not all referrals result in sales. I estimate that less than one-third of all referrals result in a sale that closes.

I have sent referrals to Mr. Bryson since he first started with us in 2003. I have not altered my handling of Mr. Bryson's referrals since January 2010 when I learned that his sister had filed an EEOC charge against Carrington Display. Because I do not track referrals, I do not know the precise number of referrals I send to Mr. Bryson each month. I do not believe his referrals have declined over time. His overall sales and overall income increased in 2010 over the 2009 levels and increased again in the first half of 2011 over the 2010 levels.

Shortly after Carrington Display received notice of Ms. Randall's charge, I mentioned in a meeting that I would be out of the office the next day because I had to meet with lawyers about Ms. Randall's charge. Mr. Bryson did not respond to this statement, nor did I expect him to. Other than this brief reference to his sister's claim, I have never discussed Ms. Randall's charge with her brother and I do not know whether he agrees with the claims she has made. Because Mr. Bryson and Ms. Randall do not work in the same office, I have not witnessed many interactions between them. I am not aware of any participation by Mr. Bryson in his sister's claims. I have not retaliated in any way against Mr. Bryson because of his sister's claim, nor has any other employee of Carrington Display.

Mike Carrington
Mike Carrington

Signed and sworn before me, a notary public for the state of Jefferson, on September 27, 2011.

Roxanne Hill
Printed Name: Roxanne Hill
My commission expires: 11/2011

2

O. Sample Mediation Statement

Mediation Statement of Matthew Bryson

Plaintiff in

Bryson v. Carrington Display, Inc.

pending in the

United States District Court for the Northern District of Jefferson

Introduction

Matthew Bryson's sister, Jennifer Randall, complained of sex discrimination by their mutual employer, Carrington Display. Carrington Display responded by cutting the sales referrals it gave to Bryson, who is paid on a commission basis. Such retaliation violates Title VII of the Civil Rights Act of 1964. Bryson seeks back pay for the income he has lost because of the reduction in referrals. Bryson also seeks institution of a record-keeping procedure tracking referrals at Carrington Display, with the records made available to all commission-based employees.

Factual background

Bryson began working for Carrington Display, a company that sells trade-show exhibit modules, in 2003. Bryson is a productive salesperson. He earned "salesperson of the month" awards at least once a year from 2004 through 2009. From 2003 until January 2010, Bryson received numerous sales referrals from Carrington Display's president, Mike Carrington.

Carrington Display hired Bryson's sister, Randall, as a salesperson in 2008. Randall was the only female in the office where she worked. Carrington Display assigned her duties not given to the male salespeople, such as making coffee and answering phones. These additional duties interfered with Randall's ability to make sales. Randall complained to her supervisor about the additional duties, but the supervisor took no action. In December 2009, Randall filed a charge of discrimination with the EEOC. Carrington Display was informed of this charge in January 2010.

At the January 2010 monthly sales meeting, Mike Carrington made a derogatory reference to Randall's claim. After this sales meeting, Carrington cut the number of sales referrals he gave to Bryson each month. While Bryson had previously received several referrals every month, months now pass in which Bryson receives no referrals. The few referrals he does receive are for labor-intensive but small dollar-value orders. While Bryson has managed to increase

1

his income over the past year-and-a-half through his own sales efforts, his income would have been higher if Carrington Display had not cut his referrals.

Bryson has heard comments demonstrating that Carrington intentionally reduced the number of referrals he gave Bryson to punish Bryson for the charge of discrimination filed by Randall. On one occasion, Bryson heard Carrington tell another salesperson that he was giving the salesperson the referral because the customer would appreciate having a "real man" on the job. On another occasion Carrington told Bryson he would not send a customer to him because the customer "wouldn't want to deal with a complainer."

Bryson filed suit against Carrington Display, alleging retaliation in violation of Title VII, in February 2011.

Claims and defenses

- **Bryson's claim:** Bryson sued Carrington Display for violating Title VII of the Civil Rights Act of 1964. Specifically, Bryson asserts that Carrington violated the anti-retaliation provision of Title VII by reducing the quantity and quality of referrals given to Bryson in retaliation for the sex discrimination charge filed by Bryson's sister.

- **Carrington Display's defenses:** Carrington Display has not asserted any affirmative defenses. It claims that Bryson's third-party retaliation claim is not cognizable under Title VII. It also denies reducing Bryson's referrals and asserts that Bryson's evidence is inadequate to show that Carrington Display took an adverse action against Bryson.

Contested legal issues

- **Third-party retaliation claims:** The parties disagree about whether a third-party retaliation claim can be brought under Title VII. The anti-retaliation provision of Title VII states:

    It shall be an unlawful employment practice for any employer to discriminate against any of his employees . . . because he has opposed any practice made an unlawful employment practice by this subchapter, or because he has made a charge, testified, assisted, or participated in any manner in an investigation, proceeding, or hearing under this subchapter.

    42 U.S.C. § 2000e-3 (2006). Bryson concedes that the plain language of this provision appears to require that the person asserting the anti-retaliation claim be the same person who engaged in protected activity under Title VII. Here, Bryson's sister, not Bryson, engaged in protected activity. Still, Bryson contends that the better-reasoned position is that adopted by the United States District Court for the Northern District of New York and endorsed by dissenting judges in the Fifth and Sixth

2

Circuits. These authorities recognize that an employer should not be allowed to do an end-run around the anti-retaliation provision by punishing a relative for the complaining party's conduct. The EEOC Compliance Manual also recognizes that retaliation against relatives is unlawful. While the Second Circuit has not decided the issue, it has stated in other contexts that the Compliance Manual is entitled to deference as long as it is persuasive. Bryson believes that he has a reasonable chance of getting the district court to decide the issue in his favor.

- **Adverse action:** The parties disagree about whether Carrington Display took adverse action against Bryson. Bryson contends that he now receives fewer referrals than he did before his sister filed her charge of discrimination. While Bryson's income has continued to increase through his own hard work, Bryson has received only labor-intensive, low-value referrals. Mike Carrington contends that he has not altered his method for distributing referrals. Carrington's comments that he was giving another salesperson a referral because the customer would appreciate having a "real man" on the job and that he would not send another customer to Bryson because the customer "wouldn't want to deal with a complainer" will help Bryson prove that Carrington did, indeed, take adverse action against Bryson.

- **Evidence of damages:** Because Bryson's income has continued to increase, Carrington Display contends that Bryson has inadequate evidence to prove a reduction in his referrals. While Mike Carrington has not kept records of the referrals he distributes, Bryson believes Carrington Display will not be allowed to benefit from Mike Carrington's inadequate record keeping. Bryson believes he can prove his damages by comparing the commissions he has earned from referrals to the commissions earned from referrals by his fellow salespeople over the same period.

Relief sought

Bryson seeks $87,000 in lost commissions, plus $67,000 in attorneys' fees and costs. Bryson believes that mediation provides an opportunity for the parties to reach an agreement that will prevent similar disputes in the future. Specifically, Bryson would like Carrington Display to agree to institute record-keeping procedures to track the referrals given to each employee. Bryson would like Carrington Display to agree further to make these records available to all commission-based employees so that the employees will be assured of equitable treatment. Bryson believes the increase in employee morale that would result from such a system would benefit Carrington Display.

Thank you for your assistance in our efforts to resolve these matters. We look forward to working with you at the mediation next week.

3

P. SAMPLE JURY INSTRUCTION

The complete jury charge in a case will address the multitude of issues that arise in that case. It will be composed of both standard admonitory instructions and definitions as well as instructions and definitions for the particular issues, causes of action, and defenses in the case. When parties submit their proposed jury instructions for a case, they typically submit only the case-specific instructions and definitions. Each instruction or definition is often submitted on a separate page, sometimes with a place for the judge to sign to indicate if the proposed instruction or definition will be given. The party's proposed set of instructions are submitted in one document, with an appropriate caption and title on the front and a signature line and certificate of service at the back. The following sample shows how one proposed instruction from an entire set might look.

United States District Court
For the Northern District of Jefferson

Matthew Bryson,
Plaintiff

Civil Action No. 11-CV-743

v.

Carrington Display, Inc.,
Defendant

Plaintiff's Proposed Jury Instruction on Retaliation

Plaintiff Matthew Bryson asks the Court to instruct the jury as follows:

Plaintiff Matthew Bryson claims that Defendant Carrington Display discriminated against him because Bryson opposed a practice made unlawful by Title VII of the Civil Rights Act of 1964.

In order to prevail on this claim, Bryson must show all the following:

First: Bryson engaged in protected opposition under Title VII of the Civil Rights Act of 1964;

Second: Carrington Display was aware of Bryson's opposition;

Third: Carrington Display took materially adverse action against Bryson; and

Fourth: Carrington Display took the materially adverse action because of Bryson's opposition protected by Title VII of the Civil Rights Act of 1964.

1

An action is "materially adverse" if the challenged action well might discourage a reasonable employee from supporting a charge of discrimination.

Sources: *Burlington N. & Santa Fe Ry. Co. v. White*, 548 U.S. 53, 68 (2006); *Kessler v. Westchester Co. Dept. of Soc. Servs.*, 461 F.3d 199, 205-206 (2d Cir. 2006): Kevin F. O'Malley et al., *Federal Jury Practice and Instructions* vol. 3C, § 171.25 (5th ed., West Group Supp. 2009).

Given: _____

Refused: _____

Given as modified: _____

Signed: _____   Date:_____

2

Index

48966743R00137

Made in the USA
Lexington, KY
19 January 2016